Multiverse Revolution

"Antidoxa" collection

First published in French under the title: *La Révolution Multivers. Le jumeau numérique au cœur du renouveau industriel européen* © 2023, Hermann Éditeurs. All rights reserved

Cover illustration: Wireframe rendering of turbojet engine and mirrored physical body on black background, digital twin concept, 3D rendering image. ©cheskyw, 123rf.

www.editions-hermann.fr

ISBN : 979 1 0370 3151 8

© 2023, Hermann Éditeurs, 6 rue Labrouste, 75015 Paris.

Any reproduction or representation of this book, complete or partial, made without the explicit consent of the publisher, is illegal and constitutes an infringement of copyright. Any use is strictly limited to private use or quotation as governed by French Law (loi du 11 mars 1957).

Florence Verzelen

MULTIVERSE REVOLUTION

The digital twin technology at the heart
of Europe's industrial renewal

Disclaimer

The opinions and contents expressed in this book are the sole responsibility of the author. No responsibility or liability is assumed by the publisher.

Introduction

The time of reversals: is this an opportunity for the Europe of tomorrow?

> "There is nothing permanent except change."
> Heraclitus of Ephesus

From the coronavirus pandemic to the outbreak of the Russia-Ukraine war, a series of crises has upset global balance in recent years, including recurring armed conflicts, the disruption of value and supply chains and the increasing price of raw materials. The illusion of a peaceful universe, of living happily ever after in keeping with the "doux commerce" theory, is long gone. These events have underlined the problems of strategic autonomy and European sovereignty as never before, problems that had receded into the background during the 2010s. For Europe and France, this troubled period confirmed how urgent it is for us to have a vision and an ambition for industrial transformation if we are to protect their interests and ensure their sovereignty.

Today, this is all the more critical because we are on the verge of a technological revolution that is leading to a paradigm shift—you might even call it a leap into the unknown, with all the uncertainties and opportunities this entails. Just as the emergence of the consumer Internet profoundly transformed people's daily lives, giving rise to new economic giants at the turn of the twenty-first century, the advent of the virtual industrial world is an opportunity to start afresh at all levels and in all sectors: production, healthcare, education, infrastructure. If the right choices are made in taking up this challenge, the Europeans, and the French in particular, have all the resources they need to put themselves at the fore of this movement and reestablish their leadership.

The emergence of new technologies in fields as varied as space, cyberspace, quantum mechanics or advanced medicine will enable our societies to explore new frontiers and ameliorate their relationship to the world. This doesn't mean our existence will be virtualized: on the contrary, increasing the power of the industrial virtual enterprise means improving our reality, increasing knowledge of our environment and of the consequences of our actions, and optimizing our available resources.

For European companies and governments, the real challenge is to accelerate these developments, which not only have the capacity to advance economic competitiveness but can also ameliorate people's everyday lives. The ongoing wave of innovations will provide concrete answers to the fundamental challenges of the twenty-first century: the ecological emergency, the energy transition, the demographic and urban explosion, health hazards, aging populations and the conquest of space. These radical transformations are paving the way for a series of reversals, starting with letting go of some of the certainties that governed yesterday's world.

From the post-industrial myth to the hyper-industrial world

The first reversal in thinking concerns the crucial place of industry and the resilience of Western economies. While some people predicted a transition to a "post-industrial society[1]" dominated by the prescription of goods and their conceptualization and immaterialization, we are actually entering a completely new phase in the history of capitalism, with a new dynamic that can be called "hyper-industrial": "Manufacturing, industrial sectors and digital business are now part of the same whole, and are more and more closely intertwined[2]." Within this ecosystem, the boundaries of the past are disappearing, leaving in their stead a stronger synergy between industry and services, digital technology and infrastructure projects, the virtual sphere and the world of factories. We need only think of the brazen success of Amazon, which combines the best of digital expertise (immediacy, one-click purchasing and responsive customer service) with unparalleled know-how in logistics, which lies at the heart of the industrial sector.

The guidelines adopted by some countries—and France in particular—haven't yet enabled them to adapt to this change. While the Americans and the Chinese still rely on the future of their industries, France has encouraged a fable ("post-industrial society", the model of the factory-less enterprise[3]) whose cruel moral has now become evident: by divesting ourselves of our production capacities, and by

---

1. Daniel Cohen, *Three Lectures on Post-Industrial Society* (Cambridge: MIT Press, 2008).

2. Pierre Veltz, *La Société hyper-industrielle. Le nouveau capitalisme productif* (The hyper-industrial society. The new capitalism) (Paris: Seuil, 2017).

3. This concept is also referred to as "fabless", a word coined by Serge Tchuruk, the former CEO of Alcatel, in the early 2000s.

neglecting part of our strategic infrastructures, we have cut ourselves off from our own strengths, and we have developed a series of dependencies (energy, new technologies, food, etc.) contingent on other geographical areas. From this point of view, Covid-19 and the war in Ukraine have been revelatory. They have reminded us that it's urgent to rely more on our industrial tool if we are to remain masters of our collective destiny and prepare for the future.

From the omnipotent virtual to the revenge of the real

The second reversal deals with the digital revolution and its impact on the way our societies function. Contrary to what many tech gurus may claim, we aren't being thrust into a completely virtualized world. The profusion of innovations at work can instead enable us to improve our environment by meeting the primary needs of people in the twenty-first century, including healthcare, education, sustainable growth, housing and agriculture. While the invention of the Internet and Web 2.0 went hand in hand with the digitalization of our very existence, the technologies of the 2020s can reverse this trend by enhancing our mastery of the physical world, further expanding the field of knowledge, facilitating resource management and strengthening simulation tools. In short, they will magnify reality.

We are slowly moving away from the fantasy that the future will be based only on digital applications, algorithmic life and immaterial economy. Yet this belief prevailed a decade ago, when America's star tech investor Marc Andreessen declared that software would devour the world[4]. This prophecy has partly come true, insofar as the

---

4. Marc Andreessen, "Why Software Is Eating the World", *The Wall Street Journal*, August 20, 2011.

2010s confirmed the overwhelming dominance of large platforms (GAFAM, NATU, BATX[5]) and their growing hold on our digital civilization.

But during the pandemic, this approach also showed its limitations. Like other public figures, Marc Andreessen was ultimately forced to reconsider his mantra. He expressed his dismay that Western countries seemed so powerless, so helpless in their fight against the coronavirus. The pandemic was a kind of warning for those countries, who found themselves without the capacity to manufacture what was necessary to fight it[6]. We could all see that faced with the public health crisis, neither the GAFAM platforms nor 2.0 technologies were of much help.

While the key players in the digital revolution made our daily life easier in terms of deliveries (Amazon, Uber Eats), entertainment (Netflix, Prime Video) or remote business meetings (Microsoft Teams, Zoom, Google Meet), they weren't equipped to solve our most critical and urgent challenges: the lack of medical equipment, masks, respirators or vaccines—in short, the tangible goods our societies needed most to fight the disease. There's even a certain irony to this when you consider that GAFAM had been promoting myths of transhumanism, promising to "defeat death" and revolutionize the world of medicine[7]. So far, this hasn't been the case… It wasn't GAFAM that "saved the world" from Covid-19, nor did they find answers to the population's health needs.

---

5. GAFAM: Google, Apple, Facebook, Amazon, Microsoft; NATU: Netflix, Airbnb, Tesla, Uber; BATX: Baidu, Alibaba, Tencent, Xiaomi.

6. Marc Andreessen, "It's time to build", a16z.com, 18 April 2020; David Rotman, "Covid-19 has blown apart the myth of Silicon Valley innovation", *MIT Technology Review*, 25 April 2020, www.technologyreview.com.

7. Christine Kerdellant, "Google voulait 'vaincre la mort'. L'IA devait remplacer les médecins… Où sont passés les sauveurs du monde ?" (Google wanted to 'defeat death'. AI was supposed to replace doctors… Where are the world's saviors?) Usinenouvelle.com, 2 April 2020.

The pandemic had at least the merit of raising awareness. It proved, once again, that it's impossible to do without certain means of production and industrial skills. More generally, the pandemic called into question the meaning and purpose of our technological ecosystem: are we innovating in the right direction? What's the point of having digital prowess when the essential (our health, the survival of our loved ones) is at stake? What should we do with the tremendous wave of progress we've been surfing on for the last twenty years? In short, are we finally going to create mechanisms that will be useful to the greatest number?

These questions were already raised by another billionaire investor, the caustic Peter Thiel, who declared in 2016 that "innovation in the last forty years [was] too confined to a narrow field: microcomputers, internet, software, mobile. But there's nothing really new in hardware, transport, healthcare, biotech, clean and cheap energy, space travel, underwater cities[8]." There is still much work to do in all these areas, and the potential for improvement is enormous. In each of these sectors, we don't need only digital technology but also state-of-the-art industrial know-how. This is all the more urgent because the upcoming climate crisis may call into question a number of our industrial activities and our agricultural management. Technological solutions will be essential if we are to come out on top of these challenges.

---

8. Dominique Nora, "Peter Thiel, le techno-prophète accueilli comme une rock star en France" (Peter Thiel, the techno-prophet welcomed like a rock star in France), Nouvelobs.com.

From the fourth industrial revolution
to the *Multiverse Revolution*

The third reversal deals with our view of industry. In France, the industrial sector suffers from an old-fashioned, even outdated image, one that harks back to Emile Zola's novels about the misery of the nineteenth-century working class. In France more than anywhere else, industry no longer captures people's imaginations; its appeal has been undermined, discouraging potential workers.

To promote industry and bring it closer to the needs of the people, we must position it as the backbone of a global project for developing our society. This is the main purpose of what I call the *Multiverse Revolution*—the augmentation of reality by virtual worlds, meaning a complete shift in our perspectives. By combining the best of digital technology and industrial expertise, we can expand the field of possibilities and pave the way for more sustainable, more efficient economic and social models that are also more respectful of people's well-being. Anchored in today's reality, these positive changes can delineate the contours of a digital civilization consistent with the expectations of current and future generations, a world where the virtual unlocks the potential of the real.

Of course, the risks inherent in virtualization remain very present: if we aren't careful, some people will surrender to the Internet's artificial paradise and get lost in the Metaverses, preferring their digital avatars over tangible existence. But the issues linked to the Multiverse are very different: there's a world of Metaverses that are risky, and a world of Multiverses that are desirable, in the same way there's both good and bad cholesterol. The Multiverse is meant to combine the best of the real and the virtual to improve our ecosystem. Thanks to this connection between the Metaverses and reality, thanks to this extended universe we call the Multiverse, we will be able to move freely between interconnected dimensions to improve the environment that surrounds us at all levels (individual, the city, the planet). With simulation technology (digital twin initiatives, quantum computers), we also have the opportunity to imagine, imitate and see several possible worlds or scenarios in order to choose the most desirable path for humanity's future. Perhaps we will finally create the "best of all possible worlds" that Leibniz wrote about[9]. For France and Europe, this *Multiverse Revolution* is cause for hope. If we have the ambition and give ourselves the means to make this technological leap, we will make Europe an avant-garde area that protects our population and our ecology, without freeing ourselves from the requirements of economic competition. France and Europe have an opportunity to reclaim a central place in the world, both from an industrial point of view and as a place with a social project that is different from the Asian or North American models.

The time of reversals could mean the end of giving up and the start of an era of renewal!

---

9. Gottfried Wilhelm Leibniz, *Theodicy: Essays on the Goodness of God, the Freedom of Man and the Origin of Evil,* 1710.

1.

NO APOCALYPSE, NOT NOW.
REENCHANTING INDUSTRIAL PROGRESS

> "A decadent civilization has no project other than to remain intact, as if saving itself consisted in being in turmoil about the innovations it introduced itself."
>
> Julien Freund, *La Fin de la Renaissance*
> *(The End of the Renaissance)*

In recent decades, the proliferation of industrial disasters (the nuclear accident in Chernobyl in 1986, the explosion of the Deepwater Horizon oil drilling rig in 2010, the Fukushima tragedy in 2011, the 2020 explosion in the Port of Beirut) has contributed to changing the way citizens view technological progress. As a result of these disasters and the subsequent media coverage of them, our conception of risk has evolved: it's no longer seen as the consequence of external events, subject to fate or divine will, but as an intrinsic component of our industrial societies in a context where, thanks to technological progress, the mortality rate linked to natural disasters has never stopped dwindling.

Human activities and innovations are now perceived as the main source of threats to our collective existence, which represents a genuine break as compared to previous periods[1]. The scientific faith of the Third Republic and the technical optimism of the *trente glorieuses*—which was in line with the legacy of Saint-Simonianism[2]—have been followed by the return of fears and declinist positions, as if we had entered a "post-progressive" era[3].

A farewell to progress?

These fears aren't necessarily surprising in an aging Europe that has seen its hegemony challenged by the United States and then by the rise of emerging nations. Faced with the technological power of the Americans and the Chinese, competitors bathing in the brazen successes of GAFAM, NATU and BATX, Europe seems to be lagging behind, relegated to the second tier. Less innovative than it was in the past, it has lost its place of leadership in many areas. Its populations no longer look to the future with the soul of a conqueror but remain obsessed with decline and the prospect of decadence.

A contemporary concept: the great collapse

What is of greater concern is that this pessimism also permeates a certain number of young people who represent the future of our countries. Although many in this new generation were breastfed on digital technology and are ultra-connected, they believe less and less in the virtues of

---

1. Ulrich Beck, *Risk Society: Towards a New Modernity* (London: Sage, 1992).

2. An economic and social doctrine elaborated by the Count of Saint-Simon (1760-1825) based on the perception that industrialization would inspire great advancements in society.

3. Pierre-André Taguieff, *Le retour de la décadence. Penser l'époque postprogressiste* (The return of decadence. Thinking the post-progressive era) (Paris: PUF, 2022).

science and technology to build an appealing future. The legitimate anxiety that has resulted from global warming and from questions about the human footprint on the environment have had a tendency, in fact, to reinforce criticism of progress.

One need only think of the success of the theory that everything can collapse, especially among students. Writing a book for a young audience on collapsology—a current of thought that until then had been marginalized—Pablo Servigne and Raphaël Stevens achieved great success, selling more than 100,000 copies of their first essay[4]. Other intellectuals have also surfed this wave, including the biologist Jared Diamond, one of the pioneers in popularizing this theory. Comparing the trajectory of our societies to that of vanished civilizations, he has given a great deal of support to those predicting societal collapse[5].

The collapsology craze is only one symptom among many (the popularity of survivalism, the degrowth theory, fascination with the precautionary principle…) of the growing hostility towards innovation and its essential driving force: industrial progress. We were able to see this again at the graduation ceremony for AgroParisTech in 2022, when students explained they were refusing employment that "takes part in social and ecological destruction", and called on their peers to boycott agribusiness jobs that "are waging war on the living world[6]." The YouTube video of their speech racked up thousands of views in France.

---

4. Pablo Servigne, Raphaël Stevens, *How Everything Can Collapse: A Manual for Our Times* (Cambridge: Polity, 2020).

5. Jared Diamond, *Collapse: How Societies Choose to Fail or Succeed* (New York: Viking Penguin, 2005); and *Upheaval: Turning Points for Nations in Crisis* (Boston: Little Brown and Company, 2019).

6. Youtube.com: https://www.youtube.com/watch?v=SUOVOC2Kd50.

New technologies on trial

Having to question the impact of human activities on the ecosystem is perfectly justified; wanting to change things and avoid a large-scale cataclysm, even more so. But we feel skeptical of the stance of young engineers who seem to be rejecting the very careers they studied for: shouldn't they be the first to imagine virtuous, sustainable solutions within the agrifood industry to support responsible agriculture? Does condemning industrial models lock, stock and barrel reflect a constructive and mature attitude? Will exiling yourself to the some ZAD land zone in the village of Notre-Dame-des-Landes, as some of them advocate, really change anything? These graduates had laudable intentions, but it's not sure the direction they're taking is really the one to follow…

Paul Hermelin, the president of the Capgemini consulting company, analyzed this astutely when he expressed concern about "the scope of the separation between young people and an optimistic vision of change coming through and with science[7]." Confronted with profound upheavals (climate change, the increasing threat of pandemics, job automation and robotization, the development of artificial intelligence) that are upsetting their equilibrium, our societies are putting new technologies and industry on trial. Instead of seeing them as possible remedies to the difficulties we are facing, many describe them as the matrix of our problems. While "science and technology were seen […] since the eighteenth century and its encyclopedists as bringing freedom, hope for growth and well-being[8]", they are now suspected of destroying the planet, enslaving individuals and leading us to disaster.

---

7. Paul Hermelin, *La science en procès. Sans innovation, pas de démocratie* (Science on trial) (Paris: L'Observatoire, 2021).
8. *Ibid.*

The winner of the 2022 Nobel Prize in Physics, Frenchman Alain Aspect, who shared the award with American John Clauser and Austrian Anton Zeilinger for their work on entangled particles, made a similar observation, describing the rise of an anti-scientific discourse that posits science as an enemy of the planet and asserts that returning to the state of nature would be preferable[9].

Breaking with this crude, caricatured vision is essential, because it bears the seeds of inevitable decline: in the absence of innovation and industrial efforts, we will be unable to overcome the challenges that await us. Returning to Malthusian positions or choosing degrowth would be harmful, irresponsible, even suicidal. We must fight this catastrophic approach, which is not founded on any viable alternative.

At the roots of deindustrialization

The industrial imaginary, from dust to misery

We must go even further, by making industry more appealing, more desirable—especially in France, where the mistrust of innovation is more pronounced than elsewhere in Europe and around the world[10]. Unlike other countries, France has been unable to create a sense of excitement about and desire for the industrial universe. Some international surveys show this very clearly: only 36% of the French find industry appealing, a tiny percentage compared

---

9. AFP, 7 December 2022, "Climat : le Nobel français de physique s'inquiète d'un 'discours anti-scientifique'" (Climate: the French Nobel in physics worries about "anti-scientific discourse").

10. Lexpress.fr, 27 October 2021, "Paul Hermelin : 'Il y a une singularité française dans la méfiance face à l'innovation'" (Paul Hermelin: 'There's something particularly French in the mistrust of innovation').

to the responses of the Americans (67%) and the Chinese (82%)[11]. How can we convince young people that this sector opens the door to careers that keep you feeling engaged and inspired in a country where industry's image is so tarnished?

These data are corroborated by an international study conducted jointly by the Institut Choiseul and the French group Chargeurs to compare perceptions of industry in Germany, the United States, France and Japan. While the survey showed that attitudes are evolving positively way in France, especially among the younger generation, the general image remains comparatively poor: only 31% of young French graduates consider the sector appealing and promising as compared to 35% of Americans and 55% of Germans[12].

By cultivating an image worthy of Zola's novel *La Bête humaine* (The Beast Within), some French élites and opinion leaders turned industry into a perfect foil. Neither political discourse nor the educational system has promoted the industrial ambition among younger gene-rations. "By hyperbolizing the alienation and drudgery in the productive model", they have "in a sense, actively participated in the expulsion of industry from French society. Teachers in vocational schools, for their part, have opposed the apprenticeship model. Professional high schools have massively oriented young people towards the service sector. Training centers were converted for lack of candidates. No one wanted to love industry and to defend it from the moment it was on the ground. [...] Nobody wanted to attribute positive values to industry in these years

---

11. Pierre Veltz, *op. cit.*

12. In a study carried out by the Institut Choiseul and the Chargeurs group, published in October 2018: *Perception comparée de l'industrie en France, en Allemagne, aux États-Unis et au Japon* (Comparative perception of the industry in France, Germany, the United States and Japan.)

of globalization. People, including working-class families, were left to think that a nation could be powerful by being post-industrial[13]." All of these elements have together given industry a distorted image: young people haven't heard that it offers numerous opportunities, that wages are higher than in the service sector, and that factories are the laboratories of tomorrow's world, where traditional know-how is being combined with digital modernity to give rise to the revolutions to come.

The factory, a symbolic territory abandoned

Disregarded both socially and economically, industry is also absent from pop culture and mass media. Unlike hospitals (*Grey's Anatomy, House),* lawyers *(How to Get Away with Murder, Suits*) or the police *(CSI),* the world of the factory has never been the subject of a television series glorifying its daily routine; television shows have breathed new life into cooking (*Top Chef, MasterChef)* or the life of real estate agents (*House Hunters*), a profession that was never hugely popular, but industry is absent from popular TV programs, at best ignored, and at worst relegated to an antiquated past that has no relationship to the hypermodern factories of the twenty-first century.

One of the few bright spots in this picture, which is dark, to say the least, was the success of the exhibition *Usine Extraordinaire* (Extraordinary Factory), held in November 2018 at the Grand Palais in Paris, which attracted around 50,000 visitors over a three-day period. By choosing an exceptional setting to present the industry of the future in all its facets, the organizers managed to shine a positive spotlight on industry. Such events, which

---

13. Nicolas Dufourcq, *La désindustrialisation de la France. 1995-2015* (The deindustrialization of France. 1995-2015) (Paris: Odile Jacob, 2022).

contribute to changing people's outlooks and fighting prejudices, are unfortunately still too few and far between.

French industry, from decline to revival?

In this overall context, how can we be surprised by the decline of industrial employment in France? It would take an entire book to retrace the seeming collapse of our productive system. In this respect, the advocates of collapsology would have plenty to say… The movement began in the 1970s and rapidly accelerated at the turn of the century, without the government being particularly affected: "Between 1995 and 2015, the country lost nearly half of its factories and a third of its industrial jobs. Numerous municipalities and industrial valleys were wiped off the map. Countless skills disappeared, industries disintegrated, and society as a whole turned away from industry, which was synonymous with defeat[14]." The shock was much more brutal than in other European nations. Endogenous factors (problems with competitive pay, the rigidity of the labor market, the over-transposition of European directives, education and training policies, etc.) and exogenous factors (the acceleration of globalization, the growth of emerging countries) were combined with questionable orientations (the "company without frontiers" model), giving rise to an economic and social disaster[15].

Only recently, this subject has been taken up again at the highest level, and industrial ambition has returned to the forefront with labels such as "French Fab", created in October 2017 by the French public investment bank (BPI); or the France 2030 investment plan, endowed with 30 billion euros for the period 2022-2027, intended to prioritize projects to modernize French industry; and to

---

14. *Ibid.*
15. *Ibid.*

new components including small modular reactors (SMRs), green hydrogen, digital factories, low-carbon manufacturing, low-carbon aircraft, electric and hybrid vehicles, deep-sea exploration and space exploration[16]. While it's still difficult to measure their results, these initiatives are proof of positive shifts in favor of the sector. All the actors (large groups, SMEs, startups, government agencies, local government) have realized how urgent it is to act together regenerate French industry.

The unfulfilled promise of the digital revolution

Industry has a crucial role to play in the world to come. It will be the main driver of innovation in a digital civilization that has yet to reveal all its facets and still seems incomplete. Until now, the impact of new technologies has mainly been seen in terms of lifestyle and consumption. The first digital wave was that of the B2C e-commerce, Web 2.0 and the dedication of large online platforms. These advances have redefined our daily lives and habits: widening the scope of communication and information, one-click shopping, easier mobility, the development of teleworking, the expansion of digital entertainment…

What is innovation for?

While they have undeniably had positive consequences—none of us would seriously consider depriving ourselves of the benefits of digital technology—these innovations have introduced new anxieties: the replacement of humans

---

16. Gouvernement.fr, 25 May 2022, "France 2030 : un plan d'investissement pour la France de demain" (France 2030: an investment plan for the France of tomorrow).

by machines or artificial intelligence; the uberization of the labor market; fear of Big Brother 2.0; a reduction in attention span[17] and cognitive abilities in young people. Some people predict jobs will be disappearing, while others announce the advent of a generation of idiots[18] addicted to their smartphones…

Although these criticisms may be alarmist and excessive, they also reveal a change in the perception of digital technology. After the first years of exhilaration and euphoria inspired by the discovery of an unknown territory with almost infinite possibilities, we are now experiencing a return to reality of sorts. Everyone is wondering about the true purpose and meaning of these technologies. What do they really bring to our societies, and to our collective well-being? Don't they just increase the narcissistic and consumeristic failings of modern life? Aren't they just gadgets that make no decisive contribution to the flourishing of humanity? Isn't there a risk that young generations will live only online?

These questions are also raised by economists who doubt that the digital revolution is a source of growth and improvement of the standard of living in Western countries. After Robert Gordon, who wrote about the economics of secular stagnation[19], many academics have underlined the limitations of the digital tidal wave. In France, Daniel Cohen, a professor at the Ecole Normale Supérieure (ENS), explains that "the promise of the digital revolution is not reflected in statistics for economic

---

17. Bruno Patino, *La civilisation du poisson rouge. Petit traité sur le marché de l'attention* (The Goldfish Civilization) (Paris: Grasset, 2019).

18. Michel Desmurget, *La fabrique du crétin digital. Les dangers des écrans pour nos enfants* (The Digital Idiot Factory) (Paris: Seuil, 2019).

19. Robert J. Gordon, *The Rise and Fall of American Growth: The U.S. Standard of Living Since the Civil War* (Princeton: Princeton University Press, 2016).

growth[20]", which in Europe has fallen from 3% in the 1970s to 1.5% in the 1990s and to 0.5% at in the years 2000-2010. At the same time, the incomes of 90% of Americans have stagnated or declined, despite the emergence of digital behemoths that have reaped enormous wealth, but employ very few people. As Daniel Cohen pointed out, it's as if "a small number of handsomely paid people were working to make the goods consumed by the poor free[21]." From this point of view, digital technology is not a sustainable vector of progress.

Behind these pessimistic theses is also the idea that the great inventions that transformed our planet are behind us: railroads, steam engines, telegraphs, telephones, electricity, automobiles, etc. According to Robert Gordon, the digitalization of society would be a "major but short-lived shock[22]", one that would be unlikely to revive growth, put people to work and create a ripple effect comparable to previous revolutions. In short, instead of the flying cars and trips to Mars that earlier generations imagined in the twenty-first century, we got Twitter, TikTok and Twitch…

A prelude to the industry of tomorrow

In addition to being reductive, this image of the digital revolution overlooks a decisive element: with the emergence of the industrial digital transformation, we will experience a technological take-off whose impact will be much greater than that of the Internet for the general public. We will witness changes that will reconcile individuals with

---

20. Daniel Cohen, *The Infinite Desire for Growth* (Princeton: Princeton University Press, 2018).

21. Daniel Cohen referred to American economist Edward Glaeser in his book, *op. cit.*

22. *Ibid.*

technical innovation by providing tangible solutions to the structural needs of contemporary society: healthcare, working conditions, housing and construction, smart cities, transportation, education and the environment.

These realizations will be the fruit of a phenomenon in which "occurring simultaneously are waves of further breakthroughs in areas ranging from gene sequencing to nanotechnology, from renewable energies to quantum computing. It is the fusion of these technologies and their interaction across the physical, digital and biological domains that make the fourth industrial revolution fundamentally different from previous revolutions[23]."

The general public has already seen the potential of digital transformation in the industrial sector thanks to the use of digital twins[24] to help fight against Covid-19. The vaccine was developed in about 9 months, whereas in the past, it might have taken ten or fifteen years. To achieve this, pharmaceutical companies relied on expertise that was at the crossroads of the digital sphere and the industrial world. Moderna, for example, used digital technologies to simplify the development of clinical trials for its Messenger RNA (mRNA) vaccine against coronavirus, relying on the Rave Clinical Cloud Platform with the support of Medidata, a subsidiary of Dassault Systèmes specializing in medical software. Forced to work in a hurry because of

---

23. Klaus Schwab, *La Fourth Industrial Revolution* (New York: Penguin, 2017).

24. "The digital twin is the [virtual] double of a real entity: a process, a machine, a structure, an environment, an object, a person." Applied to the healthcare field, it corresponds to "the utilization of digital technologies to reproduce situations or care environments, to teach diagnostic and therapeutic procedures and to allow processes, clinical situations or decision-making to be repeated by one or more health professionals". Jean-Claude Granry, "Les Jumeaux Numériques: un avenir majeur de la simulation en santé" (Digital Twins: a major future for healthcare simulation), *La Rev'SimS*, no. 3, December 2021.

the global pandemic, Moderna's teams found innovative solutions, particularly during phase 3 of the clinical trials, which involved 30,000 people: the "virtualization" of the study, electronic data capture, digital evaluation of the results and a centralized statistical analysis[25].

Other companies also pursued this path, including GSK, the British biopharma company, and Siemens, the German energy technology and manufacturing company, which joined forces, reducing the time spent on developing the vaccines by about a third. Precious time was saved thanks to "using a digital twin in the early phase to model processes and reduce the number of physical experiments in one or more stages of manufacturing. In production mode, this device enables the optimization of all the parameters for pharmaceutical groups as well as resolving recurring problems: with trials, many batches containing very expensive products end up being thrown away, which causes financial losses estimated at several hundred thousand euros each time. Thanks to digital twins, the failure rate is greatly reduced, which leads to substantial savings[26]." This innovation therefore benefits all users. Scientific advances that were thought impossible a few years ago are finally taking shape and revolutionizing the world of healthcare.

By combining virtual modeling, simulation and visualization tools with the use of real-life data and industrial excellence, digital twin technology promises to transform not only the medicine of the future but also a host of economic and social domains: aviation, infrastructures, metropolises, factories, etc. In a way, in the coming years, the embodiment of this new kind of industry will spearhead

---

25. www.3ds.com, July 2020, "Vaccins contre la COVID-19" (Vaccines against COVID-19).

26. Nicolas Petrovic, *La société post-digitale* (The post-digital society) (Paris: Débats Publics, 2021).

sustainable technologies that are useful to the greatest number of people, and will enrich and improve the world we live in.

In this respect, this is no longer a time for fatalism or catastrophism. We need to stop talking about the death of progress, or imagining we should be resigned to the critical challenges (pandemics, resource scarcity, global warming) that await humanity.

2.

THE METAVERSE OR THE MULTIVERSE?
IMPROVING ON THE REAL WORLD

> "I'm going to hang up this phone, and then I'm going to show these people what you don't want them to see. I'm going to show them a world without you. A world without rules and controls, without borders or boundaries. A world where anything is possible[1]."
>
> Neo, *The Matrix* (1999)

In October 2021, Facebook's parent company renamed itself Meta. The change marked a strategic shift for Mark Zuckerberg's company which aimed, as with the others in GAFAM, to diversify its activities. This initiative also included the creation of a virtual reality platform called Horizon Worlds, meant to accompany the large-scale adoption of the Metaverse by capitalizing on Facebook's 2 billion followers and Meta's subsidiary, Oculus, a virtual reality software and hardware company specializing in virtual reality headsets. In this immersive world, accessible through connected devices, users' avatars can interact with

---

1. *The Matrix* is a 1999 science-fiction film written and directed by the Wachowskis, with Keanu Reeves as the protagonist, Neo.

each other. Approximately 20 billion dollars have been invested since 2021 to give birth to this project[2].

The Metaverse: buzzword or Copernican Revolution?

The failure of Horizon Worlds

One year later, the results still haven't met expectations. While Horizon Worlds was aiming for 500,000 enrollments by the end of 2022, the goal has been reduced to 280,000. Struggling to attract participants, the platform is also having trouble holding onto them: between February and October 2021, it went from 300,000 to 200,000 according to *The Wall Street Journal*. Closer to the desert than to the OASIS—the teeming Metaverse directed by Steven Spielberg in *Ready Player One* and adapted from Ernest Cline's eponymous novel[3]—Horizon Worlds is not convincing users at the moment. These difficulties have had an impact on Meta's financial performance, with its share price falling by 23% on October 2, 2022. As for the group's value, which had crossed the 1,000 billion dollars mark a few months earlier, it fell back to much lower levels.

Like Web 3, Mark Zuckerberg's Metaverse had a difficult start. What's more, the general context isn't particularly favorable for technology stocks (especially cryptocurrencies and NFTs), which have been affected by the rise in bond rates and the decline in investments. With

---

2. Marie Terrier, "Le métaverse devait sauver Facebook, mais Mark Zuckerberg peine à convaincre" (The metaverse was supposed to save Facebook, but Mark Zuckerberg is struggling to convince people), Huffingtonpost.fr, 27 October 2022.

3. Ernest Cline, *Ready Player One* (New York: Crown Publishing, 2011).

the falling number of Facebook users and competition from social media such as TikTok, Meta has yet to find a second wind and renew its model. For the company, the year 2022 was anything but a crowning achievement. It seemed more like an *annus horribilis.*

The Metaverse or Metaverses?

From there, it's only a short step to say that the Metaverse is just a fad, an innovation doomed to failure… but this is a step we won't take. At this stage, the technology is still in its infancy. It's a bit like the Internet of the late 1990s: with its obscure interfaces, lack of usability and esoteric language, the Web 1.0 was, in its original version, a barren playground used by only a few geeks and a handful of professionals using e-mail. It had nothing in common with the fluid and abundant universe millennials have become accustomed to browsing and surfing on their laptops, tablets and smartphones.

Moreover, the concept of "the Metaverse" is evoked in the singular whereas it designates a plurality of projects and opportunities: "Today, the term is generally used to indicate the whole of virtual worlds connected to the Internet, and in particular Meta Horizon Worlds, Decentraland, VRChat and the Sandbox, as well as games where you can create your own universe: Minecraft, Roblox, Fortnite. Above all, it describes a vision of the future of the Internet where everyone will be able to interact in three dimensions, in immersive, persistent, collaborative and shared virtual spaces. The first [Metaverses] are spatial—we move in a [Metaverse]—and social: the [Metaverse] starts with two people and could include an infinite number[4]." In

---

4. Philippe Cassoulat, François Illouz, *Métavers, NFT. Décrypter le nouveau monde* (The Metaverse, NFTs. Deciphering the new world) (Paris: Hermann, 2022).

other words, the Metaverse covers a series of applications and uses (professional, recreational, educational, etc.) that we can barely glimpse for the moment. The video game industry, with its "open world"—favored by RPG (role-playing game) enthusiasts—has undoubtedly best explored this path until now.

The potential of a nascent market

Although Mark Zuckerberg has an excellent grasp of the potential of Web 3.0 and this revolution, he is probably too much in advance, and he hasn't yet found a business model that justifies the huge sums of money sunk into Horizon Worlds. This is a recurring problem for most new entrants in an emerging or consolidating market. In this case, McKinsey estimates that the Metaverse could have a 5-trillion-dollar impact on the global economy by 2030, the equivalent of Japan's GDP. This prediction, which seems quite high and even overly optimistic, takes into account the consequences of the democratization of the Metaverse in areas as diverse as "product marketing, customer commitment, retail, brand loyalty, customer service, recruitment, training, digital twins, tourism[5]." It's easy to understand why this technology arouses so much hope and covetousness.

In addition to being a visionary, Mark Zuckerberg is a businessman who clearly understood the interest of investing in this field before others. He is now, in one way or another, preparing his next move. In this market, many companies will be able to compete: the same skills and the same level of technological precision will not be required for learning, remote medicine or video games.

---

5. *Ibid.*

In 2023, all these promises can naturally seem far away. Metaverses still lack specific and useful uses, a pitfall that Google Glass ran into in 2013, despite an important intuition: enriching the physical world through data and digital. But due to the lack of concrete applications (except for those proposed by Google) for the general public, the project was abandoned. There's no doubt the Web of tomorrow will be more immersive, more collaborative and more intelligent. In the near future, we will all study in the equivalent of digital worlds to accelerate learning in school or at work by facilitating the appropriation of new intellectual or manual knowledge. Technological barriers—such as the cost or lack of practicality of V/R headsets—will be overcome. Simple glasses will be enough to enter these connected worlds and enjoy a virtual experience as close as possible to the real thing.

First steps for the Metaverses

Conclusive attempts have already been explored in this direction for several years. This is particularly true of the Rafale flight simulators, which enable users to learn and perfect their flying and other techniques specific to military operations, in conditions similar to those in theaters of operation. Developed by Sogitec, a Dassault Aviation subsidiary, these tools, which use 3D, man-machine interfaces (MMIs) and computer-generated imagery, help pilots and armed forces anticipate the situations they will face in the field: a modular simulator for specialized training and the collective training of UAV crews; mixed reality simulator for the rear cabins of helicopters, winch operators and shooters[6].... In the same way that many technologies have appeared in the military domain (GPS, microwaves,

---

6. Sogitec.fr.

Internet, Boeing 707), these innovations are destined to spread to the civilian world and find other uses.

In a completely different vein, the city of Seoul built a Metaverse in order to transform itself, by 2030, into a "future emotional city", in the words of its mayor, Oh Se-hoon. Behind this marketing formula lies a very concrete ambition: to transpose all public services (economy, tourism, culture, education) into a digital ecosystem that will simplify remote interaction with users, access to certain procedures and dialogue with citizens. Digital technology will complete the range of services offered to individuals while removing obstacles that exist in the real world (opening hours, health restrictions, reception of disabled people, etc.). The goal is also to improve the appeal of the South Korean capital and attract more visitors: "Seoul's main tourist attractions, such as Gwanghwamun Square, the Deoksugung Palace, and the Namdaemun Market, will be presented in the 'virtual tourist zone', and lost historical resources, such as the Donuimun Gate, will be recreated[7]." Here, the Metaverse is synonymous with the extension of urban territory. Better still, it also means new forms of local democracy, creating a unique place of exchange between the city and its population; it's also a way of communicating that will help attract new tourists to Seoul.

The fantasy of virtualization

These few examples confirm that future innovations will contribute to a better understanding of the world and to an optimization of the functioning of our societies

---

7. Roch Arène, "Séoul, la capitale sud-coréenne, va se déployer dans le métavers" (Seoul, the South Korean capital, will expand into the Metaverse), Cnetfrance.fr, 16 November 2021.

thanks to augmented reality, data, digital information and the possibilities offered by simulation tools. We will witness less a virtualization than an improvement and a multiplication of the real. The widespread idea that we are evolving in an increasingly virtual and immaterial world is mostly a fantasy.

Real/virtual: a disappearing boundary

Since we entered the digital civilization, it has also become part of the public debate. Beyond the myth of the post-industrial society, which has nourished the software of many decision-makers, all of our representations are influenced by this stubborn prejudice, as if we were progressively losing contact with reality, isolated behind our screens, and would be soon "lost in the Metaverse", to borrow a phrase from French politician and (unsuccessful) presidential candidate.

Following this logic, we pretend to believe that the digital world is a separate sphere, cut off from the rest of our physical activities, as if there were no continuum between the two worlds. But nothing could be further from the truth. On the contrary, the digital world and the physical world are constantly interacting to solve a number of real-life difficulties by providing a multiplication of possibilities to improve our everyday experiences. Basically, reality becomes a combination of the real and what the virtual worlds reveal in order to allow us to solve scientific, industrial or even more trivial consumer choices. This gives us an expanded playground, and better yet, will eventually enable us to make informed decisions. Let's go even further and say that the accessibility, fluidity and playfulness of the Web disrupt our vision of the real world and encourage us to transform it: we all want to find these facilities, this fulfillment and this absence of barriers in what some would call "real life." We are less interested in escaping the physical world than in reproducing the unique experience we have enjoyed thanks to the digital revolution.

Are we living in a gigantic video game?

The increasingly blurred distinction between these two spheres has tended to fuel farfetched or conspiracy theories. Taking up the speculations of the British thinker Nick Bostrom, Elon Musk claimed that there was every chance that we were living in a parallel universe, a bit like in the film *Matrix* or in Ernest Cline's novels, which depicts humanity in the year 2044, on a planet ravaged by climatic disasters, where people prefer to evolve in the Metaverse galaxy: "Before long, billions of people around the world were working and playing in the OASIS every day. Some of them met, fell in love, and got married without ever setting foot on the same continent. The lines of distinction between a person's real identity and that of their avatar began to blur. It was the dawn of new era, one where most of the human race now spent all of their free time inside a videogame[8]." In this hypothesis, we would be the simple pawns of a computer simulation elaborated by a civilization more advanced than ours[9].

This assertion enters into resonance with an imaginary world at the crossroads of science fiction and conspiracy theories, which has been reactivated by the power of social networks: what if reality didn't exist? What if the truth lies elsewhere (as in the subtitle of the series *X-Files: At the Edge of Reality*)? What if the world is only a deceptive illusion? What if we were still prisoners of Plato's Cave,

---

8. Ernest Cline, *op. cit.*

9. Raphaële Karayan, "Pour Elon Musk, ce que nous croyons être la réalité n'est qu'une simulation" (For Elon Musk, what we think is reality is just a simulation), *Lexpress.fr*, 3 June 2016.

condemned to contemplate only shadows, without ever reaching the lights of knowledge? What if mysterious entities were pulling the strings of a game of which we are just puppets? So many questions that form the irrational and superstitious reverse side of our societies, based on progress in science, technology and rationality.

The art of simulation, the key to twenty-first-century technologies

Modeling reality: an ancient but imperfect science

In truth, we have never had so many possibilities to apprehend, understand and influence the reality around us, and these capabilities will only grow stronger in the years to come, as digital and industrial innovations develop and improve. This is a major trend in the history of modern societies: the desire to model our environment in order to better control and transform it. From the first techniques designed to quantify the world (mechanical clocks, nautical charts, double-entry bookkeeping, etc.) to the invention of statistics or computer science, we have never ceased to conceive models to optimize the functioning of human organizations, with an increasing degree of sophistication: "One of the characteristic features of modernity is the questioning of inherited opinions and customs, in order to substitute them with judgments and uses deduced from a rational examination of situations. The emergence of a statistical thought is part of this aspiration to rationality, applied to the administration of beings and things[10]."

With the exponential increase of the power of computers, we have passed a milestone in our ability to model

---

10. Olivier Rey, *Quand le monde s'est fait nombre* (When the world became a number) (Paris: Stock, 2016).

reality. The objective is less to understand situations than to anticipate them, thanks to an exhaustive survey of existing data. On paper, mathematical models offer us the opportunity to build different scenarios to predict certain risks, to determine the probability that a certain event will occur or to predict the impact of a decision, whether political, economic, environmental, etc. They can also help identify diseases more quickly through artificial intelligence or predict the best possible treatment through data analysis.

The difficulty is that some models remain largely imperfect, if not simply inaccurate, despite the lightning progress of computer science, especially when it comes to new situations. We were all able to see this during the Covid-19 pandemic, when research theories (who had a decisive role on the action of the public authorities) were frequently contradicted and fueled a great deal of controversy[11]. This problem is also visible in terms of global warming predictions; climate models are "beset with myriad problems[12]", as noted by former Obama science advisor Steven Koonin. Given the number of parameters that come into play and interfere in a chaotic way, accurately predicting the climate of the next few decades is unfortunately "just a fantasy, as you might infer from weather forecasts, which can be accurate only out to two weeks or so. That is better than they were thirty years ago, largely due to more computer power, as well as to improved observations of the atmosphere that provide a more accurate starting point for the models[13]." While we need better data to anticipate the consequences of

---

11. Paul Molga, "Covid-19 : les modèles de prévision en question" (Covid-19: forecasting models in question), *Lesechos.fr*, 5 June 2020.

12. Steven Koonin, *Unsettled: What Climate Science Tells Us, What It Doesn't, and Why It Matters* (Dallas: BenBella Books, 2021).

13. *Ibid.*

climate change and to adapt to it effectively, we still face the limitations of current modeling tools.

The good news is that the technologies being developed will be a step forward. A series of innovations are beginning to emerge that will revolutionize our ability to understand and positively transform reality. These disruptions will make the art of simulation a vector of economic and social progress for the years to come.

First disruption: the virtual twin

This is the case with the virtual twin, a concept that was born under the aegis of NASA, in 1970, during the Apollo 13 accident: "The consequences and solutions of this event (the explosion of an oxygen tank and the accumulation of CO_2) were simulated on the ground and transmitted to the astronauts, allowing their miraculous rescue[14]." To assist the crew, NASA teams at headquarters conducted multiple tests using the exact replica of the Apollo capsule.

With the digital revolution, the possibilities conferred by virtual twins have been enriched. Technology companies have become pioneers in this field, including Dassault Systèmes, which, under the impetus of its Chairman of the board and CEO, Bernard Charlès, has made this tool a means of obtaining a holistic vision of simulation: the virtual twin is not limited to the object, "it is also the way it is manufactured and the way it will be used. The digital twin is an attempt to represent as closely as possible what the real is and to act on this virtual double to give it life[15]." It offers a depiction of the real world based on

---

14. Jean-Claude Granry, *op. cit.*

15. Usinenouvelle.com, 23 April 2020, "'Il faut une vision holistique de la simulation', prône Bernard Charlès, PDG de Dassault Systèmes" ("We need a holistic vision of simulation", advocates Bernard Charlès, CEO of Dassault Systèmes).

mathematical models and scientific laws. It combines the virtual, in the form of an abstract model of an object, with the real, in the form of sources, data from the enterprise, the Internet of Things, and the cloud.

For companies, this means that it is now possible to see what they want to accomplish through virtual modeling, simulation, and visualization before implementing it in reality. Real-world data feeds the virtual twin model, which is a dynamic copy used to improve all aspects of physical operations. This convergence of the virtual and the real, maintained by a continuous cycle of information between the two universes, results in a closed loop with immense benefits.

In the manufacturing industry, for example, this translates into substantial gains: improved goods and production resources; accelerated initiatives through the testing of new concepts and manufacturing methods; sustainable innovation with the simulation and evaluation of the impact or carbon footprint of a physical product before of its creation; and the optimization of resources at all stages of the manufacturing process. As such, it's unsurprising that a growing number of organizations are interested in this technology, which already promises to be revolutionary in terms of performance. According to a Capgemini study in 2022, 47% of companies are considering strategic partnerships for digital twin projects.

But the benefits of this disruption are not confined to the economic field. They find natural outlets in the health sector, as well as in the field of construction, smart cities or logistics[16]. One example is the "Living Heart" project, which brings together cardiovascular researchers, educators, medical equipment developers, regulatory agencies and cardiologists to develop and validate high-precision,

---

16. See the upcoming chapters.

personalized digital human heart models. Their goal is to design and use personalized hearts simulated in 3D for the treatment, diagnosis and prevention of heart disease[17].

Another example is the VORTHEx project, the virtual twin of a new room at the H. Hartmann Institute of Radiotherapy and Radiosurgery in Levallois-Perret, France, which is equipped with the latest Cyberknife surgical robot. With this technology, patients can experience the treatment virtually before starting it. In concrete terms, 3D simulation will faithfully reconstitute all the technical and protocol components of the treatment: the room, the robot arm, the patient's position, the conditions and the steps of the sessions. The digital twin aims to improve patient care by familiarizing them with radiotherapy. The immersive experience and the 3D simulation allow them to better understand the treatment. The stakes are high when you consider that there are 400,000 new cancers every year in France and that 60% of these patients will undergo radiotherapy[18].

Ultimately, the entire healthcare system should be transformed by the use of virtual twins, contributing to the advent of a patient-centered care model and moving towards personalized medicine. The pharmaceutical industry will increasingly develop products and treatments that are better adapted to an individual's specific situation or genes. Production processes will be continuously optimized, time-to-market reduced and production lines adapted in real time to fluctuations in demand. Virtualization of clinical trials will also accelerate the

---

17. 3dexperiencelab.3ds.com.

18. 3ds.com, "Dassault Systèmes, the H. HARTMANN Institute and the Institute Rafaël Launch the VORTHEx Project, the World's First 3D Simulator for Radiotherapy", 12 May 2022: https://www.3ds.com/newsroom/press-releases/dassault-systemes-h-hartmann-institute-and-institute-rafael-launch-vorthex-project-worlds-first-3d-simulator-radiotherapy

time it takes to release new drugs and vaccines, as was the case for Covid-19. This will finally contribute to making innovations sustainable and more efficient, as concepts can now be digitally simulated and evaluated before physical production.

Emblematic of the *Multiverse Revolution*, the virtual twin draws on the best of the digital technology pool to tackle head-on issues that concern the daily lives of twenty-first-century individuals and their real-life situations.

The second disruption: the quantum computer

The second disruption concerns quantum physics, a discipline that was born more than a century ago and which is at the origin of technologies such as LED, lasers or transistors[19]. We are currently undergoing a second revolution under the impetus of physicists studying the manipulation and entanglement of atoms[20], but also of computer scientists and engineers interested in the potential of these processes in sectors as diverse as chemistry, the environment, aeronautics, artificial intelligence and finance.

In 2023, quantum physics is no longer just the concern of a few research laboratories. This is becoming a major concern for industrialists and digital giants (Google, IBM, Atos, etc.) who are investing huge sums of money to prepare for the future. The French government is also taking up this issue with the launch of a new Quantum Plan, announced on January 21, 2021, which includes

---

19. Julien Bobroff, *Bienvenue dans la nouvelle révolution quantique* (Welcome to the new quantum revolution) (Paris: Flammarion, 2022).

20. Quantum entanglement refers to the existence of an inextricable link between two particles, regardless of the distance between them. Thus, if the state of one of them changes, the state of its "twin" changes instantaneously, as if it were one single system.

1.8 billion euros to accelerate R&D efforts and find concrete fields of application for quantum technologies (sensors, simulators, computers, communications)[21] within five years.

In addition to all this excitement, the quest for the Holy Grail should radically transform our relationship with the world: quantum computers that "could help invent new medicines, design materials with amazing properties, and even fight global warming by figuring out how to capture CO_2 [...]. Entanglement could lead to a new type of Internet or, in the field of imaging, make it possible to take 3D photos, in the dark, behind a wall[22]..." In other words, large companies and governments don't want to miss this turning point. The search for quantum supremacy is seen as a strategic challenge and is mobilizing huge resources.

The dream of the quantum computer is not new. It was first imagined in the early 1980s in a lecture entitled "Simulating Physics with Computers" by Nobel Prize-winning physicist Richard Feynman, who had already announced the advent of nanotechnology in 1959. Thanks to quantum computers, we would have simulation tools with capacities infinitely superior to our current super-computers. By moving from the bit to the qubit (the elementary unit of quantum machines), we would enter a new dimension. With about 30 qubits, it would be possible, for example, to encode all the words contained in the Encyclopedia Britannica; and with 300 qubits, it would be possible to describe all the data produced on the planet[23].

However, there is a real gap between theory and practice. At this point, the quantum computer is only a more

---

21. *Ibid.*
22. *Ibid.*
23. *Ibid.*

or less distant promise with no real usefulness. Despite announcements by Google, which designed the Sycamore microprocessor in the fall of 2019 (a 53-qubit machine), or by Chinese scientists (such as the designers of Zuchongzhi, a 66-qubit computing system), there are still numerous technical difficulties in converting these feats into tangible applications and correcting the rate of error in existing devices: "The most advanced prototypes do not work. Or rather, they stammer, like a child learning to speak[24]." The race for qubits, which is attracting media attention, has yet to produce disruptive innovations, but many companies, such as the startup Pasqal, are working on it.

What is certain is that the quantum computer represents a veritable game changer. Those who succeed in mastering this technology will have an enormous competitive advantage. It is therefore absolutely necessary to invest in this sector and to coordinate the actions of research laboratories and industrialists in order to position themselves at the forefront of this revolution.

Two illustrations, mentioned by physicist Julien Bobroff, are enough to show the disruptions the quantum computer could generate. First, the challenge of sequestering carbon in the atmosphere, one of the keys to remedying global warming; the idea would be to find a material that would allow us to extract CO_2 and turn it into methanol. Developing such an invention requires optimizing a large number of complex chemical reactions—a quantum machine could greatly improve these calculations. Second, agriculture and the negative externalities generated by nitrogen fertilizers, which constitute an environmental disaster: "To produce these fertilizers, nitrogen must be transformed into ammonia. This chemical reaction requires furnaces at over 400°C, which consume 1 to 2% of the

---

24. *Ibid.*

world's energy and emit as much CO_2 into the atmosphere [...]. With luck, a simple protein, nitrogenase, can do the same without heating nitrogen. If a quantum computer can decipher how it works, it could be enough to imitate it in a factory, and get rid of polluting furnaces[25]!" Whatever time and money will be spent to carry out these projects, it's largely worth it: there's no doubt about their contribution to the well-being of humanity. The French and Europeans must make quantum technologies a priority.

Third disruption: continuing the space adventure

The third disruption is linked to continuing the space adventure, which remains the embodiment of the government's power and modernity. The contemporary equivalent of the important discoveries of the fifteenth and sixteenth centuries, this represents the ideal of an unsurpassable conquest. It's no coincidence that Elon Musk made the colonization of Mars and of multiplanetary life a selling point for SpaceX: he knows that his ambition is a dream machine likely to attract talent, investors and the good graces of the American administration.

But what's decisive in the conquest of space is less about exploring Mars or new planets than possessing satellites whose importance is increasingly important for our life on Earth. In the age of telecommunications and geolocation, global observation systems have become indispensable for orienting our GPS, collecting information, predicting the weather or crops, studying ocean currents, knowing the level of air pollution, informing the armed forces during conflicts or, quite simply, being able to watch television.

Satellites are among our main tools for understanding and modeling reality. Like other technologies, they

---

25. *Ibid.*

give us a better understanding of our environment. The Europeans, Americans and Chinese are competing so fiercely for space because they know that this battlefield is strategic for building the world of tomorrow. Like all the vectors of the *Multiverse Revolution*, the space adventure is one of the cornerstones of mastering reality.

3.

Overcoming ecological crises. Building a sustainable future

> "The path to mass sobriety remains to be invented. The coercive path or that of rationing are socially unacceptable. On the other hand, it is not enough to put the challenge back on individual behaviors and their degree of virtue. We are faced with a problem that affects our values, but which is also a 'technical' problem about organizing our societies."
>
> Pierre Veltz, *L'économie désirable*

As part of the Green Deal and the European Commission's digital strategy, in 2022 the European Union announced the launch of the Destination Earth (DestinE) project, a virtual twin of the planet Earth. Spearheading the ecological transition, this initiative aims to achieve the goal of carbon neutrality by 2050 while at the same time combating global warming, resource scarcity, the proliferation of natural disasters and agricultural shortages, all of which are issues at the heart of the ecological crisis.

To build a sustainable future, Europe has decided to rely on digital innovation and the potential of new modeling tools. This is excellent news: faced with a challenge as complex as that of the environmental emergency, simulation technologies will be our best allies in anticipating risks, defining resilience scenarios and making the most relevant political and economic choices.

The DestinE project will be organized around a platform that will provide access to datasets, advanced computing infrastructure, software, artificial intelligence applications and various analyses. It will integrate virtual twins of planetary subsystems, such as weather, climate, food security, water or ocean biochemistry.

Through real-time observation of natural phenomena and predictive modeling, DestinE users (scientists, public and private decision-makers, innovators, etc.) will benefit from a wealth of information and calculations that can be used to make informed decisions. If used effectively, the platform could also enable the development of applications and the integration of user-specific data.

Business leaders face ecological and technological challenges

Accelerating awareness

Projects such as DestinE could provide solutions for the future of our societies. We need innovative ecological solutions in line with the reality and challenges of the economy. While some people defend a punitive and ideological approach that borders on a rearguard action, it seems, on the contrary, essential to amplify our efforts on the technological level. This ambition concerns everyone, starting with people who have a crucial role to play in the government to facilitate and accelerate the transition to a sustainable world. In all sectors and at all levels of the company, we must rethink the organization of production methods, the carbon footprint of activities, the design of products, the management of their life cycle, etc.

For example, everyone knows that "it is crucial to move towards simpler products, better proportioned to their functions. It is not a question of advocating low tech in the sense of a return to the technologies of the past, but of establishing a form of 'techno-discernment' [...] that allows us to avoid the choice between technophobic radicalism and blissful acceptance of innovation at all costs[1]." This is the main challenge facing companies in the twenty-first century: adapting their operations and technological choices to comply with ecological imperatives without losing sight of the quest for profitability. But while the objective is clear, its implementation is less simple than it appears.

The innovations linked to virtual twins offer an excellent illustration of these difficulties. When we look closely at the use cases, we realize that the benefits of these devices in the industrial sphere are immense: they reduce product development time, improve quality and manufacturing control, and use or recover resources more efficiently throughout the life cycle. On the other hand, the adoption of this technology is facing several obstacles. First, people working in industry are not always well-informed about the value of using it and the range of opportunities it offers. Secondly, they have difficulty measuring the return on their investment and the impact of sustainability on the company's profitability. On these points, there's still a lot of work to be done in order to move towards more sustainable and virtuous business models and above all, for these ideas to be embodied in the organization's leadership[2].

---

1. Pierre Veltz, *L'économie désirable* (The Desirable Economy), (Paris: Seuil, 2021).
2. Accenture, Dassault Systèmes, *op. cit.*

Reconciling sustainability and profitability

There are positive signs of change, however. Over the last few years, a growing number of industrial companies have converted to the potential of digital twins. They use them to model complex systems (cars, Smart Cities, human hearts) and simulate their functioning with a precision that allows them to go directly from the virtual model to creation, without losing years making physical prototypes or progressively improving existing designs.

These time savings and the reduction of risks associated with complex projects explain why this innovation has been used for the development of 85% of the world's electric cars, for a majority of wind turbine installations and for the creation of revolutionary pilot projects in terms of sustainability, including electric furnaces to decarbonize materials production, the first solar airplane and biomaterials in architecture. Virtual universes allow users to design, test and model new sustainable products and processes in record time. This is a focal point where the *Multiverse Revolution* is combining profitability and sustainability.

The automotive industry was one of the first to embrace this revolution. Manufacturers are under constant pressure to produce better cars that meet increasingly stringent legal requirements for safety and durability. They must also deal with consumer demands for the rapid, large-scale availability of new vehicles and personalized models. As a result, the design and development process adopted by OEMs has changed. Whereas it once involved key steps involving prototypes and physical tests, it now aims to minimize or even eliminate them. For example, crash simulation software can accurately predict detailed behaviors that are known to have a decisive influence on safety criteria. Thanks to virtual twin technologies, manufacturers can also reduce product development time by several months, accurately predict localized effects such as material and connection failures, and avoid the CO2 emissions associated with testing, and reduce the use of prototypes by 70 to 100%, which goes along with less waste of resources and cost optimization[3].

Encouraging circularity

The other advantage of these technologies is that it encourages the circular economy and the recycling of resources. It's now possible to manage the first, second and third lives of electronic objects such as smartphones. With digital twins, we can endlessly reallocate parts and imagine their future reuse. At a time when metals are scarce and the carbon footprint is becoming a critical concern, these innovations have real value. This is a key issue when you consider that in 2019, only 17.4% of the 53.6 million tons of electronic waste were properly disposed of, collected and recycled.

Take the case of a leading global computer manufacturer that set a goal to reduce the carbon footprint of its new computer by 45% and increase the use of recycled materials by 50%. By using the virtual twin, the company was able to explore many more design options and optimize product performance while meeting key sustainability indicators. Developers studied the behavior of the virtual prototype, including a wide range of scenarios for thermal and acoustic performance, as well as electromagnetic behavior. Simulation tools were used to lighten the structural parts and improve torsional and bending performance. As a result, the company was able to meet or exceed its sustainability goals: its new generation of computers has a 47% smaller carbon footprint than its predecessor, and

____

3. *Ibid.*

its shell is made of 100% recycled materials[4]. Without the virtual twin, such a feat would have been impossible.

Another example is Circularise, a Dutch startup that focuses on commercializing blockchain technology for transparency and traceability. It developed a solution that gives all value chain actors (mining companies, electronics manufacturers, collection services, recycling companies…) the opportunity to share information about product content and material flows via a QR code that provides important data for recycling, making operations simpler and more cost-effective[5].

This intelligent idea overlaps with one of the ambitions of the European Commission, which as part of the European Green Deal and the Circular Economy Action Plan (CEAP), proposed in March 2022, the introduction of a digital passport for high-tech products or products from polluting sectors such as textiles: "The aim […] is to collect data on all products sold in the EU and make this information available so that all those involved, including consumers, can better understand the environmental impact of the products they use[6]." This is an interesting way to reduce e-waste, which is growing worldwide at 4% per year, by reusing components and avoiding wastage of resources.

More generally, it's a matter of promoting a true circular economy in Europe by raising standards in terms of eco-design: by 2030, the European Commission estimates that the Green Deal could generate savings of 132 Mtoe (megatons of oil equivalent) of primary energy, which is

---

4. Accenture, Dassault Systèmes, *op. cit.*

5. *Ibid.*

6. Andreas Nobell, "Le Passeport numérique des produits facilite la transition vers une économie circulaire" (The Digital Product Passport facilitates the transition to a circular economy), *Environnement-magazine.fr*, 22 August 2022.

almost equal to the amount of gas imported by the EU from Russia (150 billion m3 of natural gas)[7]. In short, circularity is also synonymous with strengthening our sovereignty.

Aligning digitalization with sustainable development goals

Although the use of new technologies is imperative to successfully complete the ecological transition, we also need to limit digital technology's environmental footprint. The battle must be waged on both fronts to prevent the benefits of digital civilization from being wiped away by the ongoing increase in our technological needs: "On the energy front, ICTs [information and communication technologies] consume about 10% of the world's electricity, or the equivalent of the production of 100 nuclear reactors. If digital technology were a country, it would rank third among consumers of electricity, behind China and the United States[8]." This dynamic is expected to continue through 2025, with electricity consumption increasing by 5.7% per year, reaching 20% of global needs. As for greenhouse gas emissions attributable to this sector, they could rise from 4 to 8% in the coming years[9]. And what about data centers, which are very energy consuming and account for 14% of the digital sector's carbon footprint in France alone[10]?

---

7. European Commission, Commission.europa.eu, 30 March 2022, "Green Deal: New proposals to make sustainable products the norm and strengthen Europe's resource independence."

8. Guillaume Pitron, *The Dark Cloud: The Inner Workings of a Like* (Scribe US, 2023).

9. *Ibid.*

10. Senat.fr, "Pour une transition numérique écologique" (For green and digital transition), French Senate Briefing Report no. 555, 24 June 2020.

While these numbers may be alarming, there are solutions to these challenges. First, the possibility of making data centers less polluting by powering them with low-carbon energy and by creating genuine synergies between these two areas. As recommended in a French Senate report, it would be possible, for example, to use data centers for power flexibility, to store electricity from intermittent renewable energy resources[11].

In addition, the cooling systems of these data centers can be further improved and limit resource consumption. As for cloud computing technologies, which are becoming more and more sophisticated, they allow for a better pooling of servers and energy savings of up to 80%[12]. Similarly, we are witnessing the development of green coding, with programming languages and software designed from the outset to consume fewer resources.

More and more manufacturers are integrating these requirements into their production processes. This is particularly the case in the semiconductor industry[13]. Currently, a semiconductor plant can consume up to 1 TWh of energy per year and 7 to 10 million liters of ultrapure water per day, which is monumentally wasteful. To address this situation, industry leaders such as TSMC are taking proactive measures and focusing on sustainability programs[14]. Other companies are tackling the problem head-on by setting their own emissions targets. For example, Infineon Technologies plans to reduce greenhouse gas (GHG) emissions by 70% by 2025 in relation

---

11. *Ibid.*

12. Latribune.fr, 16 February 2022, "Le cloud pourrait faire économiser 80% d'énergie aux entreprises européennes" (The cloud could save 80% of energy for European companies).

13. See Chapter 6.

14. Syed Alam, "Top 5 trends to impact the semi industry in 2022", *Accenture.com*, 9 December 2021.

to its 2019 level, and aspires to achieve carbon neutrality for emissions directly under its control by the end of 2030. For its part, Intel has set a zero GHG target for 2040 with an intermediate step in 2030 of using 100% renewable electricity[15].

These developments will all promote an alignment between digitalization, energy efficiency and the goals for carbon neutral sustainability. Far from being incompatible, these requirements must be aligned by company managers so that future innovations lead to sustainable business models. In this way, we can build a sustainable future in which digital technologies will provide concrete solutions to the major challenges facing humanity.

The cities of tomorrow, emblems of sustainability?

The urban explosion, a challenge for humanity

Among these challenges are of course, the demographic explosion and the speed of urbanization around the world. According to the latest projections of the United Nations, the world's population is expected to grow from 8 billion in 2022 to 9.7 billion in 2050, peaking at 10.4 billion in 2080[16]. This growth will fuel the phenomenon of metropolitanization, as approximately 75% of the world's inhabitants, an additional 2.5 billion people, will be concentrated in cities over the next 30 years.

In the short term, no fewer than 43 million cities will pass the threshold of 10 million inhabitants by 2030,

---

15. Mckinsey.com, 17 May 2022, "Sustainability in semiconductor operations: Toward net-zero production."

16. Un.org, 11 July 2022, "World population to reach 8 billion on November 15, 2022."

most of them in Africa, Asia and the Middle East: Delhi (India) will have 39 million people, 10 million more than in 2015; Tokyo (Japan), 36.6 million; Shanghai (China), 32.9 million; Dhaka (Bangladesh), 28.1 million; Cairo (Egypt), 25.6 million; Kinshasa (Democratic Republic of Congo), 21.9 million; and Lagos (Nigeria), 20.6 million. In other words, the population influx will over a relatively short period of time, raise huge questions in terms of infrastructure, resource management and energy consumption. How can we ensure that these cities remain livable spaces for their inhabitants, and that their growth does not aggravate the ecological crisis? How can we ensure that metropolitanization is accompanied by a reduction in CO2 emissions per capita?

The advent of smart cities

If we are to meet these challenges, we need to rethink the urban framework and foster smart cities, cities conceived as places where traditional networks and services are made more efficient for residents and businesses with digital means. This includes smoother urban transportation networks, optimized water supply and waste-disposal systems and more energy-efficient ways to light and heat buildings[17]. The development of smart cities is based on three axes closely linked to sustainable development: economic growth that is better controlled so as not to destroy resources; ecological management of the environment to reduce the impact of human activities on nature and living species; and a more equitable societal organization to improve the collective quality of life[18].

---

17. Commission.europa.eu, "What are smart cities?".
18. *McKinsey.com*, 5 June 2018, "Smart cities. Digital solutions for a more livable future."

To achieve such results, at least three layers of "smartness" are required in cities: a technological foundation that includes networks of connected devices and sensors; smart applications and data analytics capable of translating raw data into alerts and actions, along with widespread adoption of these devices by cities, businesses and citizens; and effective data management to inspire better decisions and behavioral change.

Here again, virtual twin technologies can accelerate the transition and help drive smart cities. To be sustainable and resilient, the cities of tomorrow will need to be able to adapt quickly to a more informed view of the future. Analysis, visualization and simulation tools will therefore be indispensable. In addition to information linked to maps, these tools can integrate real-time data on traffic and weather, logistics networks, demographics and climate, providing all those involved with the opportunity to make informed decisions.

One of the pioneering cities in this field is Singapore, which developed its virtual twin in 2015: Virtual Singapore, a 3D city model and collaborative data platform, led by the National Research Foundation Singapore in collaboration with the Singapore Land Authority (SLA) and Govtech (the Government Technology Agency), one of the agencies of the Infocomm Development Authority of Singapore (IDA). Through sophisticated analysis of images and data collected by government agencies in real time, Virtual Singapore has made the optimization of urban functioning its priority. Virtual Singapore will ultimately enable city planners to test different answers to a wide range of problems, from population growth in a limited area to the management of scarce resources, the organization of public events or the renovation of neighborhoods[19].

The city of Shenzhen, in China, has also built its virtual double to fight against congestion in its transportation networks. The simulation of scenarios by artificial intelligence has enabled the city of 17.5 million inhabitants to reduce traffic jams by 10%, without building new infrastructure: changing the direction of traffic on certain streets and rationalizing public transport plans according to suggestions made by AI have produced very conclusive results[20]. Paris could learn from this method to manage its traffic: if the impact of street repairs and the closure of banks of the Seine had been simulated beforehand, there might be fewer traffic jams…

Also in France, some cities have decided to do things differently. Rennes, for example, relied on 3DEXPERIENCity Virtual Rennes, a cloud-based collaborative tool that facilitates the sharing of data remotely, in order to simulate, plan and manage the city and in particular, imagine the best possible urban developments.

This virtual twin technology will also be used for the reconstruction of the city of Chernihiv in Ukraine, which was devastated by Russian bombing. Thanks to satellite images and analysis of the destruction, it will be possible to simulate a future city and to precisely estimate the cost of the work needed to rebuild the infrastructures with better environmental standards.

---

19. Accenture, Dassault Systèmes, *op. cit.*

20. Elsa Bembaron, "Quand la ville crée son double numérique pour se réinventer" (When the city creates its digital double to reinvent itself), *Lefigaro.fr*, 12 August 2022.

The transformation of the construction industry

The emergence of smart cities will also be decisive in the transformation of the construction industry, which accounts for 10% of global GDP and drives a high demand for materials and resources. From an environmental perspective, commercial and residential buildings account for 40% of the world's energy demand (60% of electricity), 25% of water consumption, and about 33% of global greenhouse gas emissions, and this trend is expected to continue. According to the most recent estimates, there will be 706 cities with at least 1 million inhabitants by 2030, 30% more than in 2018.

However, the energy consumption of buildings could be reduced by 30 to 80% through the use of virtual twins in the smart city ecosystem. Simulation software, 3D modeling and real-time analysis lead to optimizing the operational performance of a building throughout its life cycle, creating a reduction in operating costs and a significant improvement in energy management. This innovation has already proven itself in many areas, including in shopping malls in China, where data from virtual twins is used to plan and execute inspections, maintenance and repairs, reduce electricity and water consumption, and reinforce safety measures for visitors[21].

The field of healthcare also experiments with this technology with digital twins in

hospitals (complex buildings par excellence), facilitating collaboration between the various departments, care coordination and the general management of the infrastructures. Faced with such health crises as the coronavirus, this enables us to imagine "different scenarios: variations in the number and size of clusters in the territory, the

---

21. Accenture, Dassault Systèmes, *op. cit.*

rate of contaminated personnel, the number of respirators available [...], in order to test the reliability of the organization[22]." At the peak of the Covid-19 epidemic, our healthcare system would have been much more stable if hospitals had been equipped with their virtual twins.

Here as elsewhere, we realize that the simplicity and ergonomics of the Web can reshape our relationship to the world. If these innovations are a vector of performance, they are above all becoming valuable devices for sustainability. The further we go along the path of digitalization, the more we will strengthen our mastery of reality and the more we will design useful solutions for the planet.

But for this to happen, France and Europe will have to give themselves the means to achieve their ambitions. If they wish to be at the forefront of the *Multiverse Revolution*, they have every interest in developing a coherent strategy for managing the precious resources that will be the key to our future: energy and talent. By valuing and capitalizing on natural and human capital, we can face the future, and once again be leaders in terms of innovation.

---

22. Sandra Bertezene, "Hôpital : les 'jumeaux numériques', un nouvel outil de simulation" (Hospitals: 'digital twins', a new simulation tool), *Blog.cnam.fr*, 25 March 2022.

4.

THE RESOURCE WARS.
UNLEASHING ENERGY'S POTENTIAL

> "Our nineteenth-century ancestors knew the importance of coal, and the enlightened man on the street in the twentieth century was well aware of the need for oil. But today, in the twenty-first century, we are unaware that a more sustainable world is largely dependent on rock-borne substances called rare metals."
>
> Guillaume Pitron, *The Rare Metals War: The Dark Side of Clean Energy and Digital Technologies*

Marked by the outbreak of war in Ukraine, the year 2022 has confronted Europe with a new crisis. Against a backdrop of rising energy costs, the Europe's dependence has become glaring. While the post-Covid economic recovery had already fueled a rise in prices in 2021 (+170% for gas) on a global scale, several combined factors have amplified this phenomenon: Russia's unilateral decision to stop supplying some European Union governments with gas; the increase in demand and prices for LNG (liquefied natural gas); the consequences of global warming, which have amplified the need for cooling and exacerbated the shortage of hydroelectric and nuclear power; the soaring price of electricity. The age of abundance is well behind us…

Are Europe and France out of energy?

A matter of sovereignty

This episode has shown that Europe must absolutely secure its supplies and strengthen its energy sovereignty by reducing its dependence on fossil fuels and limiting its imports to a minimum. The crisis experienced by the European Union has at least served as a warning: what happened with Russian gas could easily happen with Algerian or Qatari gas in the future; like other scarce resources, gas can become a geopolitical weapon. From this point of view, everything must be done to get closer to a form of energy autonomy. This seems all the more essential as the need for electricity will be exploding throughout the world and in Europe. The reindustrialization of the continent, the continued digitalization of the economy and lifestyles, as well as the increase in electricity consumption (particularly for electric cars) will all contribute to increasing the demand for electricity over the next few years.

If it continues, the energy crisis could lead to a new wave of deindustrialization. There are some grounds for optimism, however. As Nicolas Dufourcq noted, "the problem is competition, with the extremely inexpensive energy now offered by the American and Chinese markets[1]."

To guarantee its sovereignty, the European Union has two solutions. First, the development of renewable energies, whose electricity production costs are now comparable to those of coal or gas-fired power stations, but which still pose problems of intermittency and grid load. Resolving these difficulties means accelerating the development of batteries, an area that has long been neglected and where

---

1. Alexandre Devecchio, "Industrie, les raisons d'un naufrage" (Industry, the reasons for a shipwreck), Lefigaro. fr, 30 December 2022.

China has a certain advantage, particularly in the automotive sector[2]. Several projects are emerging in this area, such as the partnership between Airbus and Renault to develop a "next generation batteries" for hybrid aircraft and longer-range electric vehicles by 2030-2035[3]. Another example is the Automotive Cells Company (ACC), created in 2020, which brings together Stellantis (formerly PSA Group), Saft (a subsidiary of TotalEnergies) and more recently, Mercedes-Benz, with the support of the European, French and German governments, to develop battery cells and modules for electric cars. These initiatives demonstrate a real desire to position the EU in a market of the future.

Nuclear power: lessons and perspectives

Second, the question of nuclear power is of primary interest to France. Some twenty reactors were shut down in the fall of 2022, putting France in a very difficult position. Unlike Germany, our country could theoretically function without gas-fired power plants and defend its energy independence. Unfortunately, the sector has been partly sacrificed over the last decade. Between the early closure of the Fessenheim plant, the establishment of Flamanville 3, excessive delays in maintenance due to Covid-19 and the skill shortage, a series of bad choices have weakened this flagship of French industry.

These pitfalls were summed up in rather unkind terms by France's former high commissioner for atomic energy, Yves Bréchet, during his hearing before the French National Assembly's commission of inquiry, charged

---

2. It should be noted, however, that depending on the battery (phones, cars, wind turbines, etc.), the same technologies and the same R&D needs do not necessarily come into play, adding an additional layer of complexity.

3. Claire Domenech, "Batteries : Airbus et Renault allient leurs forces" (Batteries: Airbus and Renault join forces), *Capital.fr*, 29 November 2022.

with establishing the reasons for the country's loss of sovereignty and energy independence, in December 2022: "The country's energy policy was decided by a headless duck. The chain of public decision-making is disastrous [...]. The scientific analysis of the files is systematically ignored, crushed by the effects of the court in the service of the rulers rather than the country[4]." His observation echoes Paul Hermelin's thoughts on the harmfulness of anti-scientific discourse[5]; by listening to political activists and pressure groups who have sought to discredit nuclear energy without the slightest discernment, France has jeopardized one of its major economical assets.

These lessons should be kept in mind at a time when a new generation of technologies is emerging: SMRs (Small Modular Reactors), small nuclear reactors with a power output equivalent to or less than 300 MWe (compared to 1,600 MWe for an EPR), whose production and operating costs are much lower than those of large infrastructures. "Manufactured in the factory in the form of industrialized modules directly installable on site[6]", these SMRs can easily replace thermal power plants, serve isolated areas, support the deployment of intermittent energies and cover a multitude of needs beyond electricity production: hydrogen, heat, propulsion, desalination, etc.

---

4. *Lefigaro.fr*, 4 December 2022, "Nucléaire : l'ancien haut-commissaire à l'énergie atomique critique 'l'inculture scientifique' des décideurs" (Nuclear: the former high commissioner for atomic energy criticizes the "scientific inculture" of decision-makers).

5. See Chapter 1.

6. Connaissancedesenergies.org, 29 April 2019, "Énergie nucléaire : 'SMR' (petits réacteurs modulaires)" (Nuclear energy: "SMR" [small modular reactors]).

Digital technology for energy efficiency and resilience

As part of the France 2030 call for projects, a number of initiatives are being launched to develop SMRs. In addition to Nuward, which was designed by a consortium that includes EDF, TechnicAtome, Naval Group and CEA, a number of startups are jumping on the band-wagon to devise innovative solutions. This is particularly true of Neext Engineering, launched in Belfort in September 2022, to offer a faster approach to integrating reactors thanks to digital technology[7]. For SMRs, as with other industrial projects, the use of digital technology and virtual twins will be of great help: design optimization and cost reduction; simulation of future performance according to operational and environmental conditions; improved maintenance and safety; and training of operators and engineers.

In the field of energy, this digital power will be an accelerator of innovation and a factor of resilience. Indeed, Europe must now adapt to a new paradigm: energy systems are becoming more and more decentralized, involving more and more actors and consumers with sometimes divergent interests. The progressive insertion of means of production of new energy, including renewable energies, consumption sources such as vehicle charging and storage technologies, is changing the architecture of these systems. To manage this complexity and develop the energy mix of the future, modeling tools are now essential[8].

This is the purpose of projects like ModeliScale, which aims to simulate the operation of vast energy systems,

---

7. Monique Clémens, "NEEXT Engineering réinvente la conception digitale des centrales nucléaires" (NEEXT Engineering reinvents the digital design of nuclear power plants), Lesechos.fr, 28 September 2022.

8. 3ds. com.

taking into account different scales of time and space, multiple sources of energy production (conventional and alternative), and various forms of consumption (buildings, vehicles, storage). In partnership with Inria (National Institute for Research in Digital Science and Technology) and energy suppliers (EDF, ENGIE), ModeliScale should soon contribute to the optimization of urban energy distribution networks.

Thanks to the modeling and simulation of the most complex cyber-physical systems, this innovation will also be used in sectors such as aeronautics, building and transportation. This is a perfect embodiment of the *Multiverse Revolution*: it allows a better understanding of ecosystems "dominated by physics (nuclear power plants, mechanical systems as in robotics, heat networks, electricity distribution networks, etc.) but which have the specificity of having a computerized control[9]." Above all, it puts the potential of the virtual industrial at the service of twentieth-century city dwellers, who aspire to live in cities where energy is easier to access, where resources are less wasted and where their everyday needs (heating, electricity, green mobility, etc.) are satisfied in optimal, environmentally friendly conditions—in short, this is an excellent way to combine the expectations of companies and citizens.

---

9. Inria.fr, 5 April 2022, "MODELISCALE modélise, simule et analyse le fonctionnement des réseaux urbains de distribution d'énergie" ("MODELISCALE models, simulates and analyzes the operation of urban energy distribution networks").

"Rare earths": the oil of the twenty-first century?

Strategic resources for the digital civilization

The other challenge facing Europe and France is that of rare earths and precious metals (lithium, germanium, vanadium, antimony, platinum, etc.), ores that have taken on major importance in the context of the digital civilization. "Robotics, artificial intelligence, digital healthcare, cybersecurity, medical biotechnologies, connected objects, nanoelectronics, driverless cars.... the most strategic sectors of the economies of the future, all the technologies that will exponentially increase our computing capacity and modernize how we consume energy, our daily routines, and even our most significant collective choices will depend entirely on rare metals[10]." In other words, access to these resources is crucial for the world's major powers.

For the Europeans, the main problem lies in the places where these resources are extracted, with ten or so countries holding the bulk of the known and available resources: South Africa, Australia, Brazil, Canada, China, the United States, Kazakhstan, Russia, Chile and Peru. Within this group, China is in a very favorable position, as it dominates the value chain for rare earths, lithium, cobalt and copper. Russia is also in a very favorable position in terms of producing palladium (used in advanced defense technologies), titanium, aluminum and nickel (which is gradually replacing cobalt for hybrid cars)[11].

---

10. Guillaume Pitron, *The Rare Metals War: The Dark Side of Clean Energy and Digital Technologies* (Scribe US, 2020).

11. Institut Choiseul, "Minerais et métaux stratégiques : matière première d'une souveraineté en recomposition" (Strategic minerals and metals: the raw material of a recomposed sovereignty), November 2022.

With the demographic, urban and industrial explosion of emerging countries, the demand for rare metals is rising exponentially. By 2040, worldwide nickel consumption will have multiplied by 19; that of cobalt by 21, and that of lithium by 42. These needs will obviously involve Europe. If Europe wants to replace hydrocarbons and aim for carbon neutrality by 2050, it will need 35 times more lithium than today (800,000 tons per year), 26 times more rare earths (3,000 tons per year), and two to four times more nickel and cobalt. If we stick to the electrification of the car fleet forecast for 2035, the end of thermal cars will have an impact of a factor of six on the need for strategic metals. As for the risks of dependence on Europe, they are strikingly apparent here: China currently covers 98% of the EU's rare earth supplies, Turkey 98% of borate requirements, and South Africa 71% of platinum[12]. The same is true for France, which imports almost 100% of its lithium from Latin America, Australia and China[13].

In light of these few facts, it's easy to understand why this theme is a central preoccupation for decision-makers. Since the publication in January 2022 of the Varin report on securing supplies of mineral resources, several avenues have been outlined to strengthen the sector in France and Europe: securing metal supplies; developing a metals diplomacy; promoting the circular economy and recycling[14], etc.

---

12. *Ibid.*

13. Étienne Goetz, "La France va ouvrir sa première grosse mine de lithium" (France to open its first large lithium mine), Lesechos.fr, 24 October 2022.

14. Institut Choiseul, *op. cit.*

The revival of the mining industry in France?

An often overlooked aspect of these metals or rare earths is that they are not so rare. Many countries, including European countries, have long preferred to import these metals rather than extract them on their own soil. Among the solutions being considered, the reopening of mines in France is undoubtedly attracting the most attention. At the inauguration of the 2022 Paris Motor Show, French President Emmanuel Macron announced that lithium deposits would be exploited at Beauvoir's kaolin quarry in the Allier region, in order to prepare for the energy transition and consolidate France's sovereignty[15]. While this project, entrusted to Imerys, a specialist in ceramic products, is quite interesting, several conditions will have to be met for it to be successful: social acceptability, the profitability of the extraction and limitations on its ecological impact.

Virtual twin technology can provide guarantees for each of these issues; it is already proving its worth in Australia and Brazil, where mining activities are much more widespread than in Europe. First, by simulating the future mining site before it is built, we can overcome the reluctance of local residents and their ease their legitimate concerns. Showing them how the operation will work, how problems will be minimized and what infrastructure will be built for the future will encourage a calm, transparent dialogue with inhabitants. This is an essential prerequisite for the project to be accepted by the greatest number.

Then, thanks to 3D visualization and the presence of sensors, work within the mine can be automated using autonomous machines, thus avoiding human accidents and increasing productivity: equipment failures and downtime

---

15. Étienne Goetz, *op. cit.*

can be anticipated, as well as "other potential benefits, such as process control, asset tracking and miner safety in difficult operating environments[16]." Even better, mining can be adjusted in real time, depending on the lithium content of a deposit and on market prices; data collected onsite can inform people as to when it is profitable to pursue or stop operations. In the long term, this process could be perfected with complete modeling of the logistics chain.

Finally, virtual twins are useful for checking compliance with environmental criteria: noise, pollution, respect for biodiversity, etc. The virtual twin is also used to reconfigure the landscape with the existing machines by imagining the second life of the site and the infrastructures that will follow the mining operation to revitalize the territory and improve the quality of life for local residents.

All these elements can contribute to the emergence of the twenty-first century mine, a world that no longer has any connection to Emile Zola's *Germinal* but is based on high ecological, human and professional standards. This can become a foundation for rethinking all industrial projects in relation to their ecosystem, and in relation to all those involved. All organizations and leaders in the sector are responsible for this: in the future, they will no longer be able to think only in terms of short-term logic; their task will be to design a future world by imagining business models that are compatible with long-term sustainability and that preserve the local economic fabric, as well as considering a host of issues that go beyond mere financial interest. It will also be a way to live up to the *Multiverse Revolution* by having a plural vision of the role of businesses, their global footprint on society and the different paths they can take to find their reason for being.

---

16. Michele Witthaus, Sean Dudley, "Digitalisation de l'activité minière" (Digitalization of the mining business), Compassmag.3ds.com, 30 December 2017.

Human capital and the war for talent: the cornerstone of the technological future

Industry faces the attractiveness test and labor shortage

Like other industrial sectors, the mining sector will need a pool of skills to regenerate and prosper: "Until recently, France was known for the quality of its steel industry, welders and foundry workers, and for the multiple uses of metals in its most prominent industrial products: shipyards, automobiles, the aeronautics and space industries, nuclear power plants, high-speed trains, armaments, etc[17]." Unfortunately, with deindustrialization, the attractiveness of these sectors has partly declined. One only has to think of the "desertification" of the nuclear sector: to comply with the objectives set by Emmanuel Macron, about 10% of engineering school graduates would have to join the industry each year to fill the labor shortage (15,000 people per year, including 4,000 engineers)[18]…

It will therefore be essential to refurbish our image of these professions. The factory or mine of the twenty-first century can attract talented workers if they are perceived as they should be: as places where excellent know-how, rooted in the artisanal and industrial tradition, rubs shoulders with digital modernity to give rise to the great innovations of tomorrow, to ensure the ecological transition and to promote France's authority. The training courses related to these professions will be all the more interesting because they will be directly connected to digital technologies, and developed in a playful way:

---

17. Institut Choiseul, *op. cit.*

18. Olaf Verhaeghe, Thomas Segers, "La France va-t-elle se retrouver dans le noir cet hiver ?" (Will France be in the dark this winter?), Lecho. be, 12 December 2022.

operators and engineers will learn to perform new tasks and manage new situations within the Multiverse.

Towards a complete overhaul of the educational system?

Beyond the immediate needs of the industrial sector, the entire French educational system must be overhauled in order to catch up technologically. This system has not adapted to major digital transformations quickly enough, and many companies lack qualified profiles in digital, which penalizes their growth. Due to the inequalities between students' training and the reality of the labor market, too many positions remain unfilled. For example, "the 'Digital Skills Index', which calculates the digital maturity score of a country according to the level of professional qualification of respondents, is established at 22/100 for France—compared to 33 worldwide[19]." If we fail to tackle this problem, it will be an additional obstacle to the country's industrialization.

This is why it's essential to reinforce digital learning as early as possible in school. Students should be familiarized with digital humanities, algorithms and coding as early as possible. We must teach them to cooperate in groups in an environment where the virtual and the real coexist: the creation of websites and digital twins, collaboration through the Metaverse, etc. Several studies carried out by the Institut Montaigne have already insisted on this: "Our country, which is often resistant to reform, will not be able to enter the digital age in the long term if it does not succeed in training its young people in engineering,

---

19. Victor Merat, "Les entreprises sont confrontées à une pénurie de talents dans les métiers du numérique, selon un rapport" (Companies are facing a talent shortage in digital jobs, according to a report), Lefigaro.fr, 16 February 2022.

programming and maintenance skills. This obviously requires national education, where the rankings in PISA and TIMSS (dedicated to the sciences, in which France is at the bottom of the pack) still leave something to be desired[20]", and in which too many students are performing poorly, especially in math. We still have a small minority of very good students, but a growing number of students are underachieving. France appears more than ever to be advancing at two different speeds, with very strong discrepancies between the two. To fix these inequalities and make education a national priority, it's urgent for France to invest significantly, to put in place performance indicators for teachers (which could be a motivating factor), and to return value (not just financial) to teaching professions. In Germany, teachers are paid twice as much as their French colleagues. If we fail to adopt these measures, we will be depriving ourselves of talent and skills by abandoning students from certain neighborhoods and geographic areas.

But there are also some positive initiatives being taken: in France, the establishment of the Campus métiers et qualifications (trades and qualifications campus) label[21], and in particular since the creation of the "Excellence" category in 2018, is an innovative action helping to develop skills in industry-focused sectors. Creating networks for vocational schools in secondary school, higher education and continuing education enables us to better adapt the training offer to industry needs, as well as to develop innovative pedagogical practices, including collaborative projects between operators, technicians and engineers.

---

20. Gilles Babinet, "Quelles priorités numériques pour les années à venir ?" (What are the digital priorities for the coming year?), Institutmontaigne. org, May 12, 2022.

21. https://www.education.gouv.fr/les-campus-des-metiers-et-des-qualifications-5075.

Project-based learning approaches still need to be more widespread, and "trades and qualifications" campuses could be the perfect place to explore this.

This will also require more sustained efforts in general spending on higher education and R&D: this is around 3.5% of the GDP in France, compared to 5 to 6% for innovative countries, which limits our capacity to invest in promising sectors such as the blockchain, the Metaverse or artificial intelligence, areas where we have expertise and talent to bring to the fore[22].

Disintermediation between higher education and training?

We will undoubtedly have to go further and accept that colleges and universities are losing their centrality in people's lives. With schooling that is too long and too expensive (especially in the United States), out of step with the rapidly changing labor market, the training provided by these traditional institutions is less relevant than it once was. In addition, they are being challenged by companies like Google, IBM, Amazon and Walmart, which are creating their own certification programs to enhance the skills of their employees and recruit talent. The Mountain View company, for example, joined a consortium of 150 companies in sectors as diverse as Verizon (telecommunications), Bayer (pharmaceuticals and agrochemicals) and Accenture (consulting and technology) to ensure that those with certification find jobs among consortium members. An educational system competitive with American universities is emerging. More and more private actors are likely to choose this path, which should

---

22. *Ibid.*

coincide with a disintermediation in our higher education and training systems.

This evolution seems unavoidable if we consider that 60% of careers expected in 2030 haven't been invented yet[23] or that at the very least, most professions will undergo profound transformations over the next ten years. We can't wait until the skills acquired in college by 20-year-old students become sufficient or "cutting-edge" enough during the 40 years of their careers. Science, technology and industry are moving too fast for that. We will therefore need for individuals to undergo training throughout their lives, to become familiar with new technologies and convert to more collaborative ways of working. In a fast-paced environment where digital innovations will increase opportunities for value creation but will also be a source of uncertainty, companies will also prefer less conformist profiles, capable of breaking out of the mold and managing unexpected situations. Selection models based on academic knowledge (even encyclopedic knowledge) and the academic application of rules will be less relevant.

A report by McKinsey Global Institute on the future of work corroborates these observations[24]. With automation in the workforce and technological progress, improving peoples' skills is essential. By 2030, labor market reconfigurations will benefit the most qualified workers, mainly in STEM learning (science, technology, engineering and math), education, healthcare and law. Two types of profiles will stand out: those that rely on digital know-how such as programming, cybersecurity or development; and those that rely on socio-emotional knowledge such as empathy, openness to other cultures and knowledge transmission. Most careers will require a higher degree of expertise:

---

23. Ernst & Young jobs report, 2018.

24. Steven Smit, Tilman Tacke, Susan Lund, James Manyika, Lea Thiel, "The future of work in Europe", McKinsey Global Institute, June 10, 2020.

21 million Europeans will have to change professions and 90 million will have to acquire new skills within their professional lives. The shortage of skilled workers will be one of the main threats to Europe.

While we don't know exactly what skills we will need in 2030, we can already imagine that a number of skills will be critical, including those related to digital technology, artificial intelligence, additive manufacturing, system engineering or digital twins. Rather than focusing on jobs, why not focus on skills? One way would be to enhance the value of each skill acquired through certifications, which could be co-constructed with industrialists[25].

Human capital is the most valuable resource of the *Multiverse Revolution*. It is up to states and companies to cultivate this wealth, which is the condition for success in a world where technological upheavals are constantly changing the rules of international competitiveness. Not unlike the rare metals war, the talent war will be one of the major battles of the twenty-first century.

---

25. Florence Verzelen, *op. cit.*

5.

THE NEW STAR WARS.
PUSHING THE BOUNDARIES OF OUTER SPACE

> "After years of relative indifference following the exploits of the Apollo missions, space exploration has obviously caught the public's imagination once again, and we're shyly beginning to admit that traveling to the most lavish and farthest-flung reaches of the universe could one day come true."
>
> Pierre-Henri d'Argenson, *The End of the World and the Last God*

The month of December 2022 concluded a difficult period for the European space industry. This began in February, in conjunction with the war in Ukraine, with the suspension of Soyuz rocket launch operations in Kourou after the departure of Russia from the Guiana Space Center (CSG). In June, the European Space Agency (ESA) confirmed that the Ariane 6 project would be delayed and that the inaugural flight would be postponed until 2023. And on December 21, 2022, the light launcher Vega C was lost over the Atlantic Ocean just minutes after its launch while carrying out its first commercial mission, with two Earth observation satellites on board, Pléiades Neo 5 and 6, designed by Airbus—"a series of geopolitical (Soyuz) and technical (Ariane 6 and Vega C) challenges that blew up European sovereignty and scattered it like puzzle pieces for several months in terms of access to space[1]." In the short term, Europe no longer has space launchers, which represents a real loss of strategic autonomy[2].

The conquest of space, for what purpose?

The conquest of space is a sector that is essential to Europe's technological future. While it enables us allows to better understand life on Earth and to simulate reality, it also creates rivalry between the great powers. The "Star Wars" that seemed to be part of distant times, with the US/USSR confrontation—when Ronald Reagan evoked images of the film saga in referring to America's missile defense system[3]—has been reactivated by mining, military and especially digital issues (telecommunications, 5G, etc.). In the near future, the challenge is less about inhabiting space or colonizing Mars, as Elon Musk ambitions, but to push the frontiers of knowledge and innovation on a global scale. The space industry is at the heart of the *Multiverse Revolution*: it is an essential way to enrich life on our planet.

---

1. Michel Cabirol, "Lanceurs spatiaux : des déboires qui dynamitent la souveraineté européenne" (Space launchers: setbacks that undermine European sovereignty), *Latribune.fr*, 22 December 2022.

2. Michel Cabirol, "Spatial : et une nouvelle catastrophe pour l'Europe avec l'échec de Vega C" (Space: and a new disaster for Europe with the failure of Vega C), *Latribune.fr*, 21 December 2022.

3. The Strategic Defense Initiative (SDI), nicknamed the "Star Wars program", was initiated in the United States in March 1983 to defend against potential nuclear attacks nuclear strike from the Soviet Union.

Low-earth orbit satellites, the future of digital technology

First, the space sector is taking on strategic importance insofar as it interconnects issues related to telecommunications, cybersecurity and technologies of the future. As time goes on, space is increasingly asserting itself as the logical extension of the digital civilization.

The craze for low-earth orbit satellite constellations is a perfect example of this movement. Unlike geostationary satellites, which are located at an altitude of 36,000 kilometers and match the Earth's rotation, these constellations are deployed at less than 2,000 kilometers from the ground; composed of a multitude of devices, they are less expensive than traditional satellites, and move faster than the planet Earth[4]; and thanks to their number and their configuration, in constellations of multiple satellites, they give constant coverage, even in the most remote areas, ensuring widespread access to digital services. At a time when Web-related uses are exploding, initiatives of this type are multiplying.

Over the last few years, many companies have decided to exploit this trend. The best known, of course, is SpaceX, Elon Musk's company, which launched its high-speed Internet constellation, Starlink, in 2019. With 3,000 satellites in service (and with a goal of 40,000)[5], the network demonstrated its value during the war in Ukraine, offering digital access to disaster-stricken regions. Amazon has also begun to develop its offer with its Project Kuiper

---

4. The average speed of a satellite in low orbit is 8km/s, or nearly 28,000km/h, allowing it to complete an orbit of the Earth in less than one and a half hours.

5. Raphaël Balanieri, "Pourquoi les projets de constellations de satellites en orbite basse se multiplient" (Why low-earth orbit satellite constellation projects are multiplying), Lesechos.fr, 27 July 2022.

initiative, capitalizing on its own areas of expertise: "High-speed service could leverage Amazon's global logistics and operational footprint for customer service, while Amazon Web Services (AWS) could provide the necessary network and infrastructure to serve a diverse and global customer base[6]." If equipped with the planned 3,000 satellites, this constellation would expand Amazon's customer base while facilitating drone delivery.

In parallel, the French satellite operator Eutelsat and its British counterpart OneWeb planned to combine forces in 2023 to create a giant in the field of connectivity: the Satellite Connectivity market is a booming, and between now and 2030, it is expected to more than triple in value, reaching 16 billion dollars[7]. Thales (France), Ericsson (Sweden) and Qualcomm (United States) also announced their association in July 2022, with the ambition of offering 5G coverage to the entire planet via 600 to 800 satellites in low orbit[8].

If this energy is put in place, companies specialized in this area will have to deal with a major constraint: contrary to what most people might think, there won't be room for everyone. Space is not infinite. A race is on for the deployment of these constellations, whose importance is obvious: in addition to allowing almost universal access to high-speed Internet—a system less onerous and simpler than fiber, in the most isolated places on the planet—these next-generation satellites will accelerate

---

6. Stéphane Condon, "Projet Kuiper : Amazon prévoit deux lancements de satellites prototypes début 2023" (Project Kuiper: Amazon plans two prototype satellite launches in early 2023), *Znet.fr*, 14 October 2022.

7. AFP, 15 November 2022, "Satellites : Eutelsat et OneWeb signent 'l'accord définitif' de leur rapprochement" (Satellites : Eutelsat and OneWeb sign a 'definitive agreement' for their combination).

8. Maxence Fabrion, "Thales, Ericsson et Qualcomm vont lancer une constellation de satellites 5G" (Thales, Ericsson and Qualcomm to launch 5G satellite constellation), Lesnumeriques.com, 12 July 2022.

the implementation of certain innovations. This is the case in China, for example, where "the manufacturer [...] Geely launched nine low-earth orbit satellites (out of a target of 240) in June [2022] to improve the navigation of self-driving cars[9]." More and more car companies are joining forces with startups to develop their own micro-constellations to ensure that some vehicles are connected everywhere, even in sparsely populated rural areas, and that latency times are extremely low. These characteristics are essential for self-driving cars in open spaces.

These devices will also encourage telemedicine, in particular with surgical interventions controlled by robots and a satellite connection. In the coming years, patients living in countries whose health systems are less well-equipped will be able to benefit from care and techniques provided by the world's best institutions through remote interventions. This will contribute to making considerable progress in healthcare around the world.

The return of space geopolitics

Second, space is once again becoming more competitive between the world's most powerful countries, which has not always been the case. Everyone obviously remembers the goals of the Cold War, with the launch of the first satellite, Sputnik, by the Soviets (October 1957)—described by *The New York Times* as a "technological Pearl Harbor[10]"—and the creation of the National Aeronautics and Space Administration (NASA) by the Americans (July 1958). At the dawn of the conquest of space, the race for innovation was stimulated by the strong rivalry between the two blocks, but also by the desire for independence

---

9. Raphaël Balanieri, *op. cit.*

10. Cherkaoui Roudani, "La géopolitique de l'espace" (The geopolitics of space), Revueconflits.com, 8 December 2021.

of certain countries, such as France, which established France's National Centre for Space Studies (the CNES) in 1961, a few years before the CSG (1964).

However, this industry has also developed under the sign of international cooperation. Take for instance the Apollo-Soyuz mission, "during which, on July 17, 1975, the first handshake took place in space between an American astronaut, Thomas Stafford, and a Russian cosmonaut, Alexis Leonov[11]." It was also in 1975 that the European Space Agency (ESA) was created, which has 22 member countries and is one of the world's major players, alongside NASA (1958), the CNES (1961) and the Chinese National Space Agency (1993).

As for the International Space Station (ISS) project, it became a reality at the end of the 1990s, in a context of rapprochement between the West and Russia: it "marked the human capacity of a world at peace, in which scientific collaboration goes hand in hand with a political objective, to bring together the superpowers of the Cold War space race, Japan, Canada and the European Space Agency[12]." China, on the other hand, was excluded from this program because the United States had identified it as a possible threat to its interests in space. We were not yet at the age of technological "decoupling" and the trade war, but the seeds of the first dissensions had already been sown.

With the rise of Sino-American tensions and the return of armed conflicts between states, we are entering a period in which space technologies are once again perceived as vital intelligence, communication, command and control capabilities. Thus, "in the United States, the creation of a real armed space force independent of the traditional

---

11. Pierre-Henri d'Argenson, *The end of the world and the last god* (Seattle: First Hill Books, 2021).

12. Raffaele Mauro, Alessandro Aresu, "La nouvelle conquête de l'espace" (The new space conquest), *Legrandcontinent.eu*, 25 May 2022.

forces, the American Space Force, marked a historical discontinuity, leading to increased capacities for information collection, logistics, defense and power projection in space[13]." This was observed during the Russian-Ukrainian war through the ultra-precise images provided by Maxar Technologies, an American entity founded in 2017 and valued at approximately 2.75 billion dollars in late 2022: many of the images broadcast by the media were its satellite images of bombed cities, or showing the presence of artillery, of armed forces or of civilians[14]. The tool thus fulfilled both communication functions and a military role…

Tomorrow, Internet connections will be above all satellite-based. Space powers will be able to attack their rivals by depriving them of their observation tools, and by destroying the infrastructures that guarantee access to digital technology and connectivity. By attacking their enemies' satellites, some nations will be able to disconnect them from the Internet, depriving them of technologies and services that are fundamental to the proper functioning of society. Protecting space capabilities will be a priority in the field of defense.

The assault on extraterrestrial resources

Third, there is a growing interest in extraterrestrial minerals: although this prospect remains remote and the technical problems are legion, the idea of space mining is increasingly coveted because it could offer a solution to the scarcity of resources on Earth. Take for example the asteroid Psyche, which is about 200 kilometers wide: the quantity of metal it contains is equivalent to millions of years in the annual production of iron and nickel worldwide—a

---

13. *Ibid.*
14. *Ibid.*

considerable windfall[15]. In addition, the celestial bodies gravitating in the universe almost all contain "rare earths" (iridium, osmium, palladium, platinum, etc.), which are used in the manufacture of advanced medical equipment, digital devices or generators for offshore wind turbines.

As for the Moon, it abounds in water, in the form of ice, which is very useful for space missions. "This water, once purified, could first of all be used to fill the water needs of astronauts [...] on site, but once separated into its fundamental components (oxygen and hydrogen), it would above all supply spacecrafts with fuel (this is what the main stage of the Ariane 5 rocket uses today)[16]. In addition, the regions of the Moon that are exposed to solar winds are said to be rich in Helium-3 deposits, which could be used for future nuclear fusion reactors. This explains why so many countries (United States, United Arab Emirates, Luxembourg, Russia, India, Japan) are developing legislation regulating the exploration and exploitation of space resources. The Obama administration was one of the first to move in this direction with the SPACE Act of 2015[17].

Nothing prevents us from imagining that in a few years, we will have cleared new areas of the galaxy. We may see space tourists or explorers making trips lasting several months to the Moon or Mars. There, they will be able to collect titanium and regolith, a material found in abundance on Mars, to produce oxygen, build infrastructure (landing pads, roads, radiation barriers, etc.), cultivate plants and even manufacture the lighter and more durable rockets of tomorrow. The challenge will be to create a viable ecosystem so that people can live there in relative

---

15. Pierre Henriquet, "L'exploitation minière dans l'espace : quel potentiel ?" (Mining in space: what is the potential?), Polytechnique-insights. com, 17 May 2022.

16. *Ibid.*

17. *Ibid.*

autonomy in terms of energy, food and logistics[18]. Reality will then come close to meeting science fiction from the years 1950-1960, as in Robert Heinlein's famous novel *The Moon is a Harsh Mistress*, in which the moon becomes a penal colony of three million inhabitants that supplies Earth with food thanks to hydroponic farms[19]…

However; it will take a great deal of time and effort to actually access these resources and envisage colonization. As we saw in the film *Gravity*, in which the protagonists were performing high-risk repairs on the Hubble Space Telescope, space is dangerous. With asteroids, for instance, it will be necessary to deal with weightlessness—an environment that is not exactly conducive to drilling, mining and resource harvesting. Immense technical progress will need to be made to harvest the resources of Psyche and other celestial bodies. The same is true for the Moon, where extreme temperatures (ranging from -230 to +120 degrees Celsius), combined with cosmic rays and the damage caused by lunar dust, make for an extremely complex situation, and would be a source of numerous attacks on the human body, whose long-term effects can include cataracts and increased cancer risks.

Until now, most businesses that have embarked on this adventure have fallen flat: this is the case of Planetary Resources, a company created in 2009 that ambitioned developing a robotic asteroid mining industry and counted big names in tech (Larry Page, Eric Schmidt, Richard Branson) among its investors, but that nevertheless ran into funding problems and had to stop operations[20].

---

18. Gérald Sanders, "L'exploitation des ressources lunaires pour les missions spatiales" (The exploitation of lunar resources for space missions), *Polytechnique-insights.com*, 17 May 2022.

19. Robert A. Heinlein, *The Moon is a Harsh Mistress* (New York: G.P. Putnam's Sons, 1966).

20. Pierre Henriquet, *op. cit.*

Questioning Europe's space strategy

A matter of timing

If Europe wants to put itself at the forefront of this revolution, it must lose no time in prioritizing its goals. The conquest of space is an ultra-competitive field that necessitates quick choices and a well-defined strategy. In November 2022, the Commissioner for the Internal Market of the European Union, Thierry Breton, officially launched the Iris² (Infrastructure for Resilience, Interconnectivity and Security by Satellite), a multi-orbit constellation, in order to bring secure European connectivity to all, strengthen the resilience of telecommunication networks and reinforce the security of high-speed Internet in case of crisis or saturation of terrestrial infrastructures.

With an allocated budget of 2.4 billion euros from the EU for the period 2023-2027 plus a contribution of 750 million euros from the ESA, this project will cost a total of 6 billion euros[21]. Europe intends to add this third constellation to the European portfolio of strategic space infrastructures, along with the existing Galileo (satellite positioning) and Copernicus (Earth observation) constellations. An ambitious timetable has been set: the Iris² constellation is intended to be fully deployed by 2027.

To meet these deadlines, it will be necessary to overcome the slowness inherent in European decision-making processes and governance mechanisms: "The United Kingdom remains a member of the ESA, but because of Brexit, it will be excluded from the Iris² constellation, whose services for the military will be ultra-secure[22]" and

---

21. Véronique Guillermard, "L'Europe lance Iris2, sa constellation de connectivité souveraine" (Europe launches Iris2, its sovereign connectivity constellation), Lefigaro.fr, 17 November 2022.

22. *Ibid.*

will impose very harsh requirements for eligibility on manufacturers. Eutelsat's potential participation in this program has yet to be decided. These complexities can slow down the machine, even though there is no urgency…. In order for Iris² to happen in time, more than just launchers and satellites will be needed: agreements will have to be made with telecommunication operators in order to have satellite Internet receivers and build the adequate infrastructure. Enormous efforts will be needed to coordinate both investments and the those involved in the project.

The emergence of an innovation ecosystem at the service of space

In addition, the European Union needs to encourage the emergence of an open ecosystem conducive to innovation and cooperation between various players in the sector. Every year in France, no fewer than 50 startups venture into the space sector, all of which hope above all for support from the government and large businesses. Large businesses can be used as platforms for startups to accelerate the marketing of products, obtain more investments and become better integrated into industrial processes. The success of such cooperative ventures during the Covid-19 crisis was clear: startups (BioNTech, Moderna, Valneva, etc.) made it possible for pharmaceutical giants to develop vaccines much more quickly. The cooperation of these two worlds paved the way for a scientific miracle that would have been unthinkable a few months earlier.

In the United States, NASA has been able to cultivate a fertile ground for boosting its space program. When one thinks of the great American successes, SpaceX and its charismatic leader Elon Musk immediately come to mind. We associate the dazzling success of this program with Tesla founder's intuition and creative genius; he has managed to revolutionize technologies by launching recycled rockets. But we forget that these feats were enabled by political and economic conditions that were beyond favorable. The projects conceived by Tesla Motors, SolarCity and SpaceX have together "benefited from $4.9 billion in local, state and federal government support, such as grants, tax breaks, investments in factory construction and subsidized loans[23]." The United States government has also played a key role, responding to the demand in enormous proportions: contracts worth 5.5 billion have been made with SpaceX and enhanced the growth of Elon Musk's company[24].

Musk has "also benefitted from direct investments in radical technologies [...] by NASA, in the case of rocket technologies [...]. This shouldn't come as a surprise—the State has been behind the development of many key technologies that are later integrated by the private sector into breakthrough innovations[25]." This is what Italian-American researcher Mariana Mazzucato calls "the entrepreneurial state": the American government and the military-industrial complex have massively financed research, and the results are being tested in startups and in the business world.

Since its inception, NASA has been a catalyst for innovation. Since the time of the Apollo program, we know that it "pushed the technological envelope, requiring significant improvements in the production process of microprocessors and also greater memory capacity[26]." These advances have had a positive and wide-ranging impact on the new technology sector; NASA has been a driving force for digital technologies.

---

23. Mariana Mazzucato, *The Entrepreneurial State: Debunking Public vs. Private Sector Myths* (New York: Anthem, 2013).
24. *Ibid.*
25. *Ibid.*
26. *Ibid.*

The ongoing efforts made by the United States administration have much to do with the sector's dynamism. For example, the startup Slingshot Aerospace signed a 39-month contract with the United States Space Force (USSF) in March 2022 for its virtual twin technology, which reflects the conditions of space in real time. "The environment includes the mapping [...] of objects in orbit as well as meteorological spatial data[27]." The USSF plans to use this digital twin for war simulation exercises, in particular to visualize potential threats and nefarious acts that could occur in orbit, something that seems even more possible since Russia targeted one of its old satellites, Kosmos-1408, during an anti-satellite weapon test in November 2021. Slingshot Aerospace's Digital Space Twin also enables the simulation of various unforeseen scenarios, including the approach of unidentified objects or collisions, and its tools also help limit risk during satellite launches[28].

A chance to dream

This strategy could inspire the European Union to stay in the race, and to imagine exciting perspectives. Ever since John F. Kennedy spoke of a "New Frontier" in July 1960, we have known that the space adventure nourishes people's wildest hopes. Space is a mobilizing objective that can bring together politics, business and citizens. China was right to enhance its space program, "drawing particular attention to its activities on the Moon, thanks to the series of probes, landers and rovers in the Chang'e program as well as its new Tiangong space station, which is now operational thanks to a central module, and

---

27. Léna Corot, "Le jumeau numérique spatial de Slingshot Aerospace séduit le gouvernement américain" (Slingshot Aerospace's digital twin seduces the American government), Usine-digitale.fr, 1 April 2022.

28. *Ibid.*

which has hosted its first astronaut crews[29]. Being in space is a way to be powerful on Earth, and to consolidate a country's technological advantages while increasing the people's prestige and pride. In spite of the costs involved, many countries know that the game is worth it.

In France, where a tradition of excellence is embodied by the CNES and the Guiana Space Center in Kourou, we have a duty to carry out the space ambition at the European level and to boost innovation. Some initiatives are moving in the right direction, such as the one led by Karista, BpiFrance and the CNES, which in the fall of 2021 created CosmiCapital, a venture capital fund entirely dedicated to NewSpace. The fund has an initial investment capacity of 38 million euros to finance solutions related to fundamental technologies (deep tech) or applications related to satellite data collection (precision agriculture, frontline surveillance, etc.). In a space market that is expected to grow from 350 billion to 1,000 or even 2,000 billion dollars over the next few years, French and European startups can increase market share if they are supported in their development[30].

With famous figures such as Thomas Pesquet (a French aerospace engineer, pilot and astronaut, considered the second most popular French personality in 2022), France is also fortunate to have this industry of the future in the spotlight. A dynamic can be set in motion, one that can regenerate the EU project beyond technocratic politics, beyond the transparency issues with institutions, with citizens supporting great industrial projects that can resuscitate the European dream, making it a land of innovations and improving life in general.

---

29. Raffaele Mauro, Alessandro Aresu, *op. cit.*

30. Léna Corot, "Bpifrance, le CNES et Karista pilotent un fonds de 38 millions d'euros pour les start-up du spatial" (Bpifrance, the CNES and Karista are piloting a 38-million euro fund for space startups), Usine-digitale.fr, 19 October 2021.

6.

BACK TO BASICS. RESTORING FRENCH AND EUROPEAN LEADERSHIP

> The industrialization of war in the years following the onset of globalization after Germany's reunification, the Tiananmen Square massacre and the fall of the Soviet Union, has not been properly read. We continue to suffer from it. Worse, we have taken a direction in conflict with our strategic interests.
>
> Nicolas Dufourcq, *La désindustrialisation de la France* (The Deindustrialization of France)

The *Multiverse Revolution* represents an opportunity for France and for Europe on a global scale. After having missed the milestone of the Internet for the general public, Europe has the chance to restore international competitiveness by developing a different approach to digital civilization and industry. Until the 1990s, neither France nor Europe had to be ashamed of their technological performance; in many sectors, they were even a driving force.

European technology, from dropping out to catching up

When Europe and France were innovative

This is particularly true for France, which has long been a place for innovation, rich in scientific culture and the know-how of its engineers. Whether in the nuclear sector (the opening of the Chinon Nuclear Power Plant in 1963), in space (the launch of the Ariane 1 program in 1973), the invention of the smart card by Roland Moreno (1974), in aeronautics (the first commercial flight of the Concorde in 1976) or for railways (the inauguration of the TGV high-speed train in 1981), we have always been able to develop breakthrough technologies.

This is also the case in the telecommunications field with the Minitel, as well as the development of the Global System for Mobile Communications (GSM) standard developed by the Centre national national d'études des télécommunications (CNET, the ancestor of Orange Labs), the Deutsche Bundespost and Scandinavian operators: they have succeeded in superseding the Americans and imposing a new standard[1].

We could also mention the introduction of the World Wide Web in 1989, at the European Organization for Nuclear Research (CERN) laboratory in Geneva, led by two computer scientists, the British Tim Berners-Lee and the Belgian Robert Cailliau, who wanted to enable scientists from all over the world to communicate instantaneously. Theoretically, France and Europe were perfectly equipped to face the digital era.

---

1. Jean-Marc Bally, Xavier Desmaison, *Junk Tech: How Silicon Valley Won the Marketing War* (Paris: Hermann, 2021).

Europe, looking at the digital tsunami

Unfortunately, this beautiful process broke down at the dawn of the twenty-first century, when another world had to be invented. The democratization of the Internet was followed by the age of Web2, social networks, mobile applications and digital platforms: a universe that sanctified the crushing domination of the Americans (GAFAM, NATU), who expanded their technological hegemony and their soft power through Silicon Valley, but also of the Chinese (BATX), who developed their own ecosystem by relying on their vast domestic market and a phenomenal economic boom. Much has already been written on this subject, and on the growing digital tech gap in Europe.

As confirmed by a report of McKinsey published in July 2022, "Europe exhibits a growing technological gap compared with the United States and, in certain sectors, China. This gap, which was initially linked to the slower adoption of digital tech, is now widening in a dozen technological fields that are crucial for future competitiveness, such as artificial intelligence, automation and biotechnology. [...] The shift in Europe's position is already being reflected in business competitiveness indicators. Between 2014 and 2019, large European companies (+1 billion dollars in annual sales) were 3 points less profitable than their counterparts in the United States. Between 2014 and 2019, large European companies (+1 billion dollars in annual revenues) were 3 percentage points less profitable than their American counterparts; their revenues grew 40% more slowly, and their investments and R&D spending have been respectively 8% and 40% lower than those of their American counterparts[2]." Regarding quantum

---

2. Clarisse Magnin-Mallez, Eric Hazan, Jean-Christophe Mieszala, Alexandre Ménard, Sven Smit, "Donner un nouveau souffle au modèle de croissance inclusive et durable de l'Europe et de la France" (Giving

computing, five of the top ten technology companies are almost all located in the United States and four are in China, with none in the European Union. For 5G, which represents the future of connectivity and conditions the large-scale dissemination of certain innovations, China captures nearly 60% of external funding, with the United States at 27% and Europe at only 11%. In terms of AI, the United States attracted 40% of this funding over the period 2015-2020, compared to 32% for Asia (including China) and 12% for Europe[3].

Over the last decade, Europe has seemed to be watching these developments happen, hesitating about what strategy to adopt. Should the GAFAMs have been more severely sanctioned? Should we be trying to create the equivalent of a Google or a European NASDAQ? Should we be giving more support to our own digital champions (especially in public markets) even if it means compromising the sacrosanct principle of free competition? Unfortunately, faced with the digital tsunami, the French and Europeans have spent more time asking questions than providing answers.

But this gap is not insurmountable. Within the framework of a *Multiverse Revolution* placed under the sign of digital transformation and ecological transition, we are witnessing a profound mutation of our economy and our industries. Our ability to adapt to this new paradigm, by directing our investments towards the sectors of the future in order to create future European giants, constitutes one of the keys to Europe's competitiveness.

---

new impetus to the inclusive and sustainable growth model of Europe and France), Mckinsey.com, July 2022.

3. Sven Smit, Magnus Tyreman, Jan Mischke, Philipp Ernst, Eric Hazan, Jurica Novak, Solveigh Hieronimus, Guillaume Dagorret, "Securing Europe's competitiveness: Addressing its technology gap", Mckinsey.com, 22 September 2022.

In this field, the time for procrastination and questioning is over. We need to act now.

What are the priorities for a digital Europe?

The sovereign cloud: a fundamental building block

This is first and foremost the case in terms of digital sovereignty, which consists in creating digital champions by supporting innovation and the growth of actors in this field. We know of greatly successful examples in Europe such as Dassault Systèmes, SAP or Capgemini, but they are far from numerous enough, nor are they large enough compared to the American tech giants. This sovereignty must also include data. Europe is now dependent on services and tools outside the continent for a majority of its digital activities. More than 80% of its data is hosted by non-European service providers, mainly American. AWS, Microsoft Azure and Google Cloud alone account for more than two-thirds of the European market.

If we want to guarantee European sovereignty, we need to set up a governance system that guarantees control of our data and ensures secure connectivity. We need to create a legislative framework that will encourage investments, which will enable us to create European alternatives to GAFAM. These are the things at stake in the common European data spaces currently under discussion, as well as the various sovereign cloud projects, such as Numspot.

In October 2022, Docaposte (the digital subsidiary of La Poste), Dassault Systèmes, Bouygues Telecom and the Banque des Territoires signed an alliance combining their expertise and strengths in a 100% French industrial consortium in order to create Numspot, a company dedicated to developing of a complete range of European cloud, sovereign cloud and trusted cloud services. This project is intended primarily for French economic and institutional players in need of solutions: the financial sector (banks, insurance companies), healthcare (hospitals, etc.) and the public sector (government, local authorities, operators)[4].

Launched in France in 2023, Numspot ambitions to expand into the European market and become the benchmark for trusted cloud services, thanks to reliable, secure technology that complies with French and European data hosting standards[5]. Its objective is to guarantee the highest level of industrial reliability and security, with data operated exclusively in France. Beyond the trust infrastructure, Numspot's objective is to offer a sovereign technological platform with software solutions and services that meet the expectations and constraints of sensitive sectors.

In the long term, this should give rise to a European reference ecosystem, positioned at the highest level worldwide, including software publishers, digital services companies and startups. Numspot will work with research laboratories, such as the French Institute for Research in Computer Science and Automation (Inria), to accelerate French and European technological innovation[6].

---

4. 3ds.com, 26 October 2022, "Docaposte, Dassault Systèmes, Bouygues Telecom et la Banque des Territoires s'allient pour proposer une offre de référence dans les services de cloud de confiance" (Docapost, Dassault Systèmes, Bouygues Telecom and Banque des Territoires join forces to offer a benchmark in trusted cloud services).

5. In France, the SecNumCloud standard was developed in 2016 by the French National Agency for Information Systems Security (ANSSI), and "enables the qualification of cloud computing service providers, more commonly referred to as 'the cloud', with the objective of promoting, enriching and improving the offer of trusted service providers for public and private entities wishing to outsource the hosting of their data, applications or information systems." Ssi.gouv.fr.

6. 3ds.com, *op. cit.*

By positioning itself more quickly than Bleu (Microsoft Azure, Orange, Capgemini) and S3ns (Google Cloud and Thales) on a sovereign cloud market estimated at 4.5 billion euros, and growing by 25% per year[7], Numspot expects to get a head start, to create a certain number of new standards and play a role in of a fundamental challenge for Europe's future: the preservation of its digital sovereignty and strategic autonomy.

The ecological transition, a technological opportunity

Europe's second asset lies in its ability to put digital transformation at the service of the ecological transition, a field in which it has considerable advantages: on average, per capita CO2 emissions in Europe are half of those in the United States. In the field of clean technologies (known as cleantech), Europe is more dynamic than most other places in the world. Europeans hold 38% more patents than American companies and more than double the number of Chinese in this specific sector. Moreover, these mature technologies have a higher degree of penetration among Europeans. Although China remains a formidable competitor, particularly regarding photovoltaic panels and electric-car batteries, Europe can still capitalize on its know-how and expertise[8].

Digital technology is an extremely powerful means of consolidating this asset and combating climate change. A study published jointly by Accenture and Dassault Systèmes showed that five use cases of digital twins in five

---

7. Francis Manens, "Numspot, cette alliance 100 % française qui vient bouger les lignes du cloud de confiance" (Numspot, the 100% French alliance that is moving the lines of trust in the cloud), Latribune.fr, 26 October 2022.

8. Sven Smit, Magnus Tyreman, Jan Mischke, Philipp Ernst, Eric Hazan, Jurica Novak, Solveigh Hieronimus, Guillaume Dagorret, *op. cit.*

industries from now until the year 2030 would eliminate the equivalent of one year's worth of emissions around the world in all transportation sectors[9]. If applied on a larger scale, from an environmental perspective, the effect of digital technologies could be spectacular.

Creating the right conditions for Europe to move ahead of the rest of the world could enable it to reconcile climate and technology requirements. In this context, the Sustainable Product Initiative (SPI) launched by the European Commission in late 2020 is particularly interesting, as it introduced the concept of a digital passport. This would accompany a certain number of products in guaranteeing their intrinsic longevity, whereas until now, in certain sectors such as electronics, programmed obsolescence has been the norm. We would therefore go far beyond eco-design, which consists of designing products with sustainable materials to enable analysis of the product's sustainability over the entire life cycle. Approaches of this type are now possible thanks to advanced platforms such as 3DEXPERIENCE.

In the coming decade, every company, regardless of its sector of activity, will have to transform itself to become green and sustainable. Making Europe digital is an essential step towards achieving the common climate and environmental objectives set out in the European Green Deal, while at the same time strengthening the resilience of European industry.

Everyone is aware that the "technological backwardness of Europe and France would constitute a considerable risk if it were to continue and increase. But there is nothing inevitable about it. Bridging the gap in these technologies represents a challenge of 2,000 to 4,000 billion euros in additional annual added value by 2040. At a time when

---

9. See Chapter 3.

environmental and social issues are becoming more important, this potential would offer Europe considerable room for maneuver[10]." To get back into the race with the United States and China, it will be essential to make strategic investments in areas that determine Europe's autonomy.

The semiconductor industry, a strategic investment

In this respect, semiconductors are an essential part of the global technological competition. From connected cars to the Internet of Things, from industrial equipment to communications and defense systems, semiconductors are a key resource for digital civilization and the *Multiverse Revolution*[11]. To put it simply, they are, in a sense, the brains of modern electronics. Their exponential power—commonly referred to as Moore's Law—has accompanied the progress of advanced technologies such as artificial intelligence, quantum computing, green energy and medical devices. Nowadays, a simple Smartphone has a computing power largely superior to that of NASA's computers at the time of man's first steps on the Moon in 1969[12]. From a more technical point of view, a semiconductor is a substance, usually a solid chemical compound or element, that can conduct electricity under certain conditions but not others, which makes it a good medium for controlling electric current[13].

On the side of technology companies, semiconductors have become a differentiating factor. Many tech giants

---

10. Clarisse Magnin-Mallez, Eric Hazan, Jean-Christophe Mieszala, Alexandre Ménard, Sven Smit, *op. cit.*

11. Vincent Deltrieu, Loïc Lietar, "Semi-conducteurs : comment faire rayonner l'Europe" (Semiconductors: How to make Europe shine), Lesechos.fr, 8 December 2022.

12. Semiconductors.com, May 2021, "Building America's innovation economy."

13. Source: KPMG.

such as Apple, Tesla, Google and Amazon are now making their own ASIC (application-specific integrated circuit) chips specifically for their own products and applications. This allows them to better control the integration of software and hardware while differentiating themselves from the competition. This is the case, for example, with Amazon and Graviton processors. Similarly, Google Pixel Smartphones use Tensor, the first chip designed by the Mountain View firm to bring artificial intelligence capabilities to its range of cell phones. As for Apple's MacBook Pro 2021, it was designed from M1 chips developed by the company internally. In any case, these companies believe they can differentiate themselves technologically by making custom chips that meet the specific requirements of their applications rather than using the same generic chips as their competitors[14].

The main challenge for Europe is to rebuild a competitive semiconductor industry. Between 2000 and 2021, Europe's share of global semiconductor production fell from 24% to 8%, a sharp decline that discloses a real danger for European technological independence[15]. This challenge has become all the more intense as the resurgence of geopolitical shocks disrupts value chains. Semiconductors are considered a core technology for digital transformation and the arms race, and are at the heart of the Sino-American rivalry and of the voracity in Taiwan, which accounts for 59% of world production.

In addition, Europe has long been more restrictive than its competitors in terms of public support for industrial production. Traditionally, the EU has preferred supporting research and innovation rather than industrial production in order to guarantee the integrity of the single market

---

14. Syed Alam, *op. cit.*

15. Institut Montaigne, March 2022, "Semiconductors in Europe: the return of industrial policy."

and the rules of free competition. Conversely, China, the United States, Japan, Taiwan, and South Korea have all engaged in massive government action to ensure the competitiveness of their domestic semiconductor ecosystems[16]. Just think of the Chips and Science Act signed on August 9, 2022, which provided 52.7 billion dollars in funding for research and manufacturing of semiconductors in order to bring more business to American soil.

In the race for semiconductors, Europe can nevertheless count on certain major strengths. With three major integrated device manufacturers (STMicroelectronics, Infineon and NXP), the world leader in photolithography (ASML), a dynamic startup scene and leading research centers in nanoelectronics (IMEC, CEA-Leti, Fraunhofer), there is plenty of fertile ground. To go further, it will be essential to step up R&D efforts and to re-industrialize a sector that has been decreasing over the last twenty years[17]. In this perspective, the Chips Act presented by the European Commission in February 2022 represents an interesting advancement.

With a budget of 45 billion euros, this plan aims to double Europe's production capacity (20% of world production by 2030) but also to make the rules for state aid more flexible in order to support the sector: "Chips that bring innovations in computing power, energy efficiency, environmental gains and artificial intelligence will be able to benefit from this public aid[18]", which covers a wide range of electronic components. If the path to

---

16. *Ibid.*

17. *Ibid.*

18. Maxence Fabrion, "Chips Act : les pays de l'UE s'accordent sur un plan à 45 milliards d'euros" (Chips Act: EU countries agree on a 45 billion euro plan), Lesnumeriques.com, 24 November 2022.

making Europe "a world leader in semiconductors[19]"—as Thierry Breton and the Commission hope—a first step has already been made. This is a prerequisite if we want to shine in the *Multiverse Revolution*.

Cybersecurity, the foundation of digital civilization

The other key factor for success lies in strengthening our cybersecurity capabilities, a field where there is still a great deal of room for improvement. With digitalization, we are witnessing the rise of hybrid threats that put not only the sovereignty of states but also manufacturers' resilience in danger: "Hybridity is a relatively recent concept, but it includes such classic means of destabilization as deformation-manipulation of opinion or sabotage, with the formidable assistance of current technological means and vectors (information networks, cyberspace, drones). [...] On the cyber level, resilience, the protection of servers (governmental, industrial, financial, emergency, energy, etc.), as well as the preservation of an unaltered information environment, must more than ever be a priority for the government, in order to guarantee conditions for the functioning of our society and the cohesion of the nation[20]." In recent years, countless companies have fallen victim to large-scale hacking and computer attacks on critical infrastructures: the derailment of the tram network in Lodz, Poland, after being hacked by a teenager; a virus attack on the computers of the Aramco oil group in Saudi Arabia; the attempted poisoning of Florida's supply of

---

19. Ec.europa.eu, 8 February 2022, "EU Chips Act : le plan de l'Europe pour redevenir leader mondial des semi-conducteurs" (EU Chips Act: Europe's plan to become a world leader in semiconductors again).

20. Thibault de Montbrial, "La France face au risque d'une menace hybride" (France faces the risk of a hybrid threat), Lefigaro.fr, 20 October 2022.

drinking water[21]; the theft of 200GB of data from the Bouygues Construction network in January 2020, with a demand for ransom (ransomware); a cyberattack against Colonial Pipeline in May 2021, causing a shutdown of the fuel pipeline from Texas to New York.… This list could go on and on, as these acts of cybercrime have become commonplace. In France alone, over the period 2020-2021, these attacks were multiplied by four[22]!

For all states and companies, finding firewalls for these attacks is an absolute necessity. The requirements for cybersecurity is now estimated at 5,700 billion euros world-wide. In France, we are fortunate to have world leaders and companies recognized for their expertise: Orange Cyberdéfense, Thales, SopraSteria, Airbus CyberSecurity, Tehtris or YesWeHack; "this solid base constitutes the hidden part of a lively and innovative private ecosystem [made up] of numerous SMEs, startups and scale-ups[23]." In addition, large industry groups are looking for cyber-security solutions before the product-development and design phase in order to secure their value chain and customers. This subject is taken very seriously by groups such as Dassault Systèmes and is reflected in the continuous increase in the skills of teams dedicated to cybersecurity.

In Europe, the strategic reflection on cybersecurity shouldn't be limited to defensive aspects. At a time when this problem is being prioritized by companies, we would be well advised to imagine solutions and standards that would allow European actors to compete internationally. As explained by the Institut Choiseul, it would be desirable to consolidate a high-level cyber offer "made in Europe"

---

21. Nicolas Petrovic, *op. cit.*

22. Institut Choiseul, June 2022, "La cybersécurité, préalable à toute souveraineté économique" (Cybersecurity, a prerequisite for economic sovereignty).

23. *Ibid.*

as a veritable alternative to foreign solutions and a long-term competitive advantage.

From this point of view, it would be necessary to ensure the establishment of a "common base of principles and criteria for 'sovereign' cybersecurity solutions that would stand out at the global level: respect for the framework of public liberties; transparency of financial flows and regard for the rule of law against terrorism and money laundering; respect for data and the RGPD; recourse to European solutions; a majority share of European technical teams and developers[24]", etc. Europe's vocation is not to imitate the United States and China in order to exist in the digital war. On the contrary, it has every interest in promoting values, norms and standards that will differentiate its industrialists and digital entrepreneurs on a global scale. The restoration of French and European leadership requires this aggressive approach.

More generally, we need a solid technological framework to inhabit the Multiverse and protect citizens in each of the spaces (physical, digital, augmented reality, etc.) where they evolve. In order for these innovations to permeate the population, issues of trust and security are essential. The *Multiverse Revolution* is not limited to its technological or economic dimension: it primarily concerns individuals who will have the opportunity to improve their daily lives if they take advantage of the tools offered by the industrial sphere.

---

24. *Ibid.*

Conclusion

Living in the multiverse

> "Technology is a tool. That is true whether it's a hammer or a deep neural network. Tools don't decide what happens to people. We decide."
>
> Andrew McAfee, Erik Brynjolfsson,
> *Machine, Platform, Crowd: Harnessing Our Digital Future*

United States/China/Europe: what technological paradigms?

Until now, the digitalization of our economy and our lifestyles has essentially been influenced by the American tech giants. The entrepreneurs of Silicon Valley have prospered by selling us a promise, that of a humanity freed from its main evils (disease, crime, pollution, etc.) thanks to digital innovation. In this respect, there would be a sort of "application" for each problem. Better known as "technological solutionism[1]", this belief has all the hallmarks of an ideology that invests the Internet and digital devices with an almost magical power. But despite some

---

1. Evgeny Morozov, *Pour tout résoudre, cliquez ici! L'aberration du solutionnisme technologique* (To solve everything, click here! The aberration of technological solutionism) (Limoges: FYP Editions, 2013).

genuine achievements, the revolution still feels incomplete. The first 100%-automated smart cities look more like dystopian environments than Gardens of Eden 2.0. As for the major challenges linked to climate change, they are far from having been solved by the champions of digital technology. The dream of a better world has not yet been fulfilled by the prophets from Silicon Valley…

In parallel to the meteoric rise of American platforms, everyone has seen the ascent of Chinese companies, the BATX, which have benefitted from extremely favorable conditions in their development. In addition to a huge domestic market, these companies benefit from government support, unlimited access to personal information and an absence of ethical rules in the use of data. Characterized by a "techno-utilitarianism[2]" that frees itself from individual liberties, the Chinese ecosystem is a closed universe that supports its leaders' political ambitions and looks like an "Orwellian drift[3]." But unlike the American model, the Chinese model seems difficult to transfer to the rest of the world—even though in the West, the young generation surfs on TikTok or uses Xiaomi Smartphones.

Faced with these two dominant paradigms, Europe must chart its own course, without naivety and without betraying its values. On the one hand, we must be aware that our technological gap endangers the sovereignty of our states, the health of our economies and the future of our populations. Without a massive effort in certain sectors, we are indeed in danger of suffering a definitive discrepancy. On the other hand, it's essential to develop a vision of the future and of digital civilization that contrasts with the American or Chinese approach. In order to compete internationally, France and Europe must take a different

---

2. Kai-Fu Lee, *I.A. La Plus Grande Mutation de l'histoire* (A.I. The Greatest Mutation in History) (Paris: Les Arènes, 2019).

3. Pierre Veltz, *L'économie désirable* (The Desirable Economy), *op. cit.*

path, by putting innovation at the service of individual and collective well-being. Innovation should not be seen as an end in itself but as a means to create a more sustainable, harmonious and inclusive society.

The *Multiverse Revolution* lies at the crossroads of industrial progress and virtual devices, offering us a unique opportunity to achieve this goal. If we focus on technologies that improve our mastery of reality and expand the scope of our knowledge, we can give rise to what Pierre Veltz has called a "desirable economy", namely an economy that creates jobs, reduces our carbon footprint and finds new growth drivers. Such things "reside in particular in the immense field of extending people's capacities (in relation to healthcare and education, in short) and of reinventing our shared living spaces (cities, new collective and territorial organizations allowing healthier, more autonomous lives). Individuals—their bodies, brains, emotions—and what could be called the 'ecumene', that is, the Earth made habitable: these are the two components of the economy of the future[4]." The industrialization of France and Europe can be the catalyst for this ambition: thanks to simulation and modelling tools (virtual twins, Metaverses, quantum computing, space, etc.), we can not only improve the performances of our businesses, but also encourage the emergence of advanced medicine, increase healthy life expectancy, make cities more livable, prevent natural disasters and most of all, rethink our education system.

---

4. *Ibid.*

An education in digital tech and data

I would like to underline this point: education will be a fundamental parameter for the future of our societies. By moving into the Multiverse, individuals will have an enriched life experience, where the boundaries between the digital and physical worlds may blur, inviting people to juggle between reality, augmented environments and Metaverses. Such a universe will multiply the range of possibilities, but will also be more difficult to understand for those without the required skills (coding, digital humanities, ability to master man-machine interfaces, etc.). To face these major transformations, we will need citizens who are better qualified and better prepared on the intellectual and technical levels. The risk lies less in the fact that some individuals lose contact with reality—as in *Les liens artificiels*, a French novel in which the young hero, Julien, prefers to live in the *Antimonde*, a revolutionary Metaverse that makes it possible to realize his craziest dreams[5]—rather than in part of the population's inability to adapt to this digitalized ecosystem. There is a key challenge here that public governments must urgently take up.

By inhabiting the Multiverse, we will also be expanding our digital identity, leaving more traces and learning to trust technologies whose existence we would not even have suspected a few years ago. These developments obviously raise huge questions in terms of public liberties and ethics: how can we protect privacy and individual data? Can simulation and modeling tools replace human decision-making processes? Does the ideal of optimization put us in danger of dehumanization?

Rather than being a source of anxieties, these questions should be seen as an expression of European technological

---

5. Nathan Devers, *Les liens artificiels* (Artificial Links), Albin Michel, August 2022.

identity and a basis for the model to be built. In fact, Europe is the only region in the world that attaches so much importance to data protection. Far from being a hindrance, this concern can be an asset in defining the relationship of our societies and citizens to digital transformations. This began with the General Data Protection Regulation (GDPR)—which foreign companies have already adopted—and has continued with the Data Act, which allows users, consumers and professionals to better benefit from the data they produce, particularly with regard to connected objects (the Internet of Things).

By extending this movement, Europe could encourage each of us to be more responsible for our data and to freely choose the companies to which we wish to entrust it, in order to derive value from it. In this area, we are only at the beginning of a large-scale change: with practice, experience and learning, European citizens should gradually become owners of their data and choose solutions in line with their personal values and aspirations. This sensitivity to data could become a comparative advantage over the United States and China.

Ruptures and false fears

Furthermore, we shouldn't pretend that the optimization of traffic and transport will inevitably lead to a Chinese-style system or digital dictatorship… What new technologies can bring, starting with virtual twins, are informed decision-making processes that take into account as many scenarios as possible, and inform both governments and citizens about the consequences of a given choice. This will undoubtedly be an excellent antidote to the demagogic promises and unrealistic projects that discredit the actions of our political leaders. The more we have the reflex to use these digital tools to help us make decisions, the more opportunities we will have to improve the world around us. But we will remain masters of our destinies. Virtual twins, artificial intelligence and other applications will never give us a goal; they will remain a tool to draw several possible futures and help us reach the ambitions we collectively set for ourselves. We will always be free to chase pipe dreams, take the wrong direction or misjudge the future.

Similarly, as individuals, we will always have control over how we use these innovations. No one will be forced to optimize their entire schedule down to the last detail or to entrust the selection of their romantic partners to algorithms. Such concepts can seem legitimately frightening, even absurd... What the *Multiverse Revolution* gives us is the opportunity to enrich our daily lives, to facilitate certain tasks and to access services (healthcare, transportation, education, etc.) that meet our needs as closely as possible. This doesn't mean we will abdicate our comprehension, our free will and our intelligence.

All technological breakthroughs and scientific advances bring with them their share of fantasies and irrational fears. In Plato's time, some people accused writing of damaging memory and weakening the mind. In the early days of the railroad, others thought that steam trains crisscrossing our countryside would frighten cows and turn their milk sour. At the dawn of the Internet, the Web was seen only as a network of hackers, neo-Nazis or pedophiles[6]. And in the age of artificial intelligence and ChatGPT, some now predict that human labor will be replaced with machines...

What History teaches us is that human societies have always learned to tame these major transformations, to cohabit with instruments and methods they had been unaware of, thus making the world more habitable. Sooner

---

6. Grégor Brandy, "Comment la France voyait internet en 1997" (How France saw the Internet in 1997), Slate.fr, 13 April 2017.

or later, fears will dissipate when the benefit/risk balance tips to the positive side. The *Multiverse Revolution* can't escape this: although it will undoubtedly bring inventions and evolutions that elude our current forecasting models, it will certainly coincide with great progress in our lives.

In a period of technological breakthroughs, we need new intellectual software more than ever. Let's reenchant industrial progress by no longer listening to the speeches of the prophets of the apocalypse, of decline and of the "Great Collapse"! Reindustrialization and investment in the innovations of the future (sovereign cloud, semiconductors, cybersecurity, space, artificial intelligence) are the best ways to meet the challenges of the century, the first of which is the absolute necessity of building a sustainable world. Neither degrowth nor rejecting science will save us from large-scale catastrophe.

The growing sophistication of simulation tools (virtual twins, quantum computing, satellites) offers a unique opportunity in this respect. These tools will enable us to gain a better understanding of our environment and provide excellent solutions in all areas, whether they concern the lives of businesses or individuals: optimizing resources, using low-carbon energy, fighting global warming and pollution, relieving congestion in cities, improving people's well-being through education and healthcare. The only risk that France and Europe runs is letting others capitalize on this immense potential for change by missing out on a transformation whose impact will be equal to, if not greater than, the invention of the Internet.

A thousand miles away from the fantasies about virtualizing the world and developing Metaverses, the *Multiverse Revolution* is a powerful movement that puts the best of digital and industrial technologies to work for our extremely real existence, for our common future. Let's embrace it fully!

TABLE OF CONTENTS

www.ingramcontent.com/pod-product-compliance
Lightning Source LLC
Chambersburg PA
CBHW062227150726
47991CB00006B/2464